SHALL WE DANCE

The Life of Ginger Rogers

Sheridan Morley

WEIDENFELD & NICOLSON
London

For Rosie and Sam Leon, and in memory of John Kobal

By the same author
A Talent to Amuse (the first biography of Noel Coward)
Review Copies: London Theatres 1970-74
Marlene Dietrich
Oscar Wilde
Sybil Thorndike: A Life in the Theatre
Gertrude Lawrence: A Bright Particular Star
Gladys Cooper
Tales from the Hollywood Raj: The British in California
Shooting Stars: London Theatres 1975-83
Katharine Hepburn
The Other Side of the Moon (the first biography of
David Niven)
*Spread a Little Happiness: The First 100 Years of the
British Musical*
Elizabeth Taylor
Odd Man Out (the first biography of James Mason)
Our Theatres in the Eighties: London Theatres 1983-89
Audrey Hepburn
Robert, My Father

and as editor:
The Noel Coward Diaries (with Graham Payn)
Noel Coward and his Friends (with Graham Payn and
Cole Lesley)
Theatre '71, '72, '73, '74
The Theatre Addict's Archive
The Autobiographies of Noel Coward
Punch at the Theatre
The Stephen Sondheim Songbook
The Theatregoer's Quiz Book
Bull's Eyes (the memoirs of Peter Bull)
Out in the Midday Sun (the paintings of Noel Coward)
The Methuen Book of Theatrical Short Stories
The Methuen Book of Film Stories

for the stage:
*Noel and Gertie, Spread A Little Happiness, Before the
Fringe*

Text © Sheridan Morley 1995

First published in Great Britain in 1995 by
George Weidenfeld & Nicolson Ltd

The Orion Publishing Group Ltd
Orion House
5 Upper Saint Martin's Lane
London, WC2H 9EA

A catalogue reference is available from the British Library

ISBN 0 297 81671 3

Designed by Anthony Cohen

Typeset by Deltatype Limited, Ellesmere Port, Cheshire

CONTENTS

Slightly forsaken, somewhat folorn
Rather resembling a startled faun,
Puckish and wistful, electric, neat,
Scaling the heights on their dancing feet -
Other performers might gladly share
The motto Per Ardua ad Astaire

(Picturegoer, 1943)

LIFE

ASTAIRE & ROGERS DO THE YAM

AUGUST 22, 1938 **10** CENTS

CHAPTER ONE

"Everything Fred did, I did backwards and in high heels"

The morning after she died, on 25 April 1995 at her home in California at the age of eighty-three, Britain's two leading broadsheet newspapers, The Times and the Daily Telegraph, led their front pages with the same colour photograph of Virginia Katherine McMath dancing with Frederick Austerlitz. By the time the photograph was taken, from the 1949 film Barkleys of Broadway, the pair had long been known as Fred Astaire and Ginger Rogers, the most celebrated and distinguished dancing duo in the history of motion pictures, perhaps in the history of the world.

The photograph was taken from their last screen appearance together, and their first in a decade. It was within a relatively short period - between 1933 and 1939 - that Astaire and Rogers made the other nine musicals with which they were forever to be linked and associated, from Flying Down to Rio to The Story of Vernon and Irene Castle. All were in black and white, and most told the same story: boy meets girl, boy dances with girl, boy nearly loses girl, boy dances with girl, boy gets girl.

The partnership may have been made some way from heaven, but it was magical and electrifying. Fred and Ginger were always much greater than the sum of their combined parts, and as one of Hollywood's most astute historians, Katharine Hepburn, once noted, that was for a very simple, good reason: "He gave her class, she gave him sex appeal."

I only ever saw Ginger on stage once, when she came to London in 1969, to the Theatre Royal, Drury Lane, to play the title role in Jerry Herman's Mame. For those of us who had seen Angela Lansbury in the Broadway original a few years earlier, the London production was a considerable and rather tacky disappointment, but there could be no doubting the star quality of the leading lady. Precious few actresses make their West End debuts at fifty-eight billed on the posters as "legendary", and she was, I guess, unlucky to have been around in the same seasons as such genuine Broadway legends as Carol Channing and Barbra Streisand.

When she came over again, a year or two before she died, to sell her memoirs, I recorded the last full-length BBC radio interview she ever gave. Already in her

Doing the Yam: Fred and Ginger in Irving Berlin's 1938 Carefree.

Ginger at 18 months with the father she never really knew, William Edding McMath.

eighties, a somewhat cranky old bat in a wheelchair, she almost appeared to be taking part in a drag version of *The Man Who Came to Dinner*. All traces of the elfin, ethereal figure who danced across a hundred staircases had vanished, and our conversation, admittedly, was not helped when she recounted the fact that all of her five husbands had been heavy drinkers. As if from elsewhere in the room, I suddenly heard myself asking, "But were they when you married them?", in one of those moments when you somehow disengage the time-lock mechanism in the brain that usually, and mercifully, delays the pronouncement of whatever you are thinking until you have had a split second to consider its suitability.

To her credit, she remained no more irritable than she had been before we started the interview. Considering the question for a moment, since it must have been relatively new to her, she eventually answered "some".

Ginger at sixteen, the first professional photograph.

She then began, briskly and sometimes quite bitterly, to recall what evidently had not been an altogether easy or even rewarding life – until, of course, it came to the steps in time.

Her early childhood had many of the qualities of the B movies into which her later career would all too often sink when she was trying to escape the long shadow of Fred's top hat, white tie and tails. She was born 16 July 1911 in the small town of Independence, Missouri; her father, Eddins McMath, was an electrical engineer who had met her mother, Lela Emogene Owens, in a Kansas City dancing school. They married on Lela's eighteenth birthday, at least partly because the Owens family were about to move on to Utah. A first child died in infancy, the second was Ginger and their last was stillborn. The marriage soon began to disintegrate under domestic and economic pressures, and Lela went to work as a local newspaper reporter. A devout Christian Scientist, she was to be the

"Sing Out Louise": Mother and daughter on the Hollywood trail.

driving force in Ginger's life, equating what was good for God with what was good for her little girl, and living long enough to make her first Atlantic flight in time to see that little girl, at almost sixty, make her Drury Lane debut.

By the time Ginger was two years old, her mother had already begun to see the little girl's potential, and had even managed to get them both photographed for display in the lobby of the new Missouri State Building as "the modern Madonna and her Child". Father was, however, not pleased with the modern Madonna, at least not when she

started divorce proceedings and removed their child to a hotel in Ennis; one night he simply kidnapped little Ginger and took her to live with him in St Louis. But Lela was not about to lose her little girl; she hired a private detective, had them traced, and within weeks Eddins appeared in court on charges of baby-snatching and reckless behaviour. As a result his visiting rights were drastically curtailed, Lela's divorce went through without difficulty, and Ginger hardly ever again saw her father, who died prematurely less than ten years later.

Neither for a while, did she see a lot of the

mother who was to dominate so much of her later life and career. Needing to earn money for herself and her daughter, Lela left Ginger (the name now established thanks to a little cousin unable to pronounce Virginia) with her own parents, while she headed to the *Kansas City Post* where, as a reporter, she began to write local stories and then short stories, one of which won a contest for conversion to a screenplay – the winner received a trip to Hollywood.

Thus by the time Ginger was five, her mother was already in California working on silent-screen scripts for Theda Bara. Lela even took part in a World War One recruiting picture which was shown in Kansas City, where the grandparents were still looking after her little girl. "They took me to the cinema to watch mother's moment in the movie," Ginger recalled years later, "I was not a very bright child, and waited in the movie-house for several minutes after the picture ended, hoping that mother would simply walk out from behind the screen."

A psychiatrist would probably be happy to explain the subsequent failure of five

Winsome, lose some: Ginger in her Vaudeville days.

By the time Ginger was two years old, her mother had already begun to see the little girl's potential, and had even managed to get them both photographed for display in the Missouri State Building as "the modern Madonna and her Child".

marriages, and an obsessive devotion to her mother and Christian Science (in roughly that order) on these early years when Ginger felt utterly abandoned by both of her parents. The alternative showbiz truth is that (like Mary Martin, with whom Ginger was at primary school) what we have here is a tough little hoofer perfectly capable of making her own career and life decisions, and uninclined to analyse them too deeply.

By the time she was ten, Ginger was already in professional dance class, much encouraged by her mother, who had now reappeared as a reporter on the *Kansas City Post*. There was also a new man in their lives, John Logan Rogers, whom Lela married in 1922 and divorced seven years later, though not before he had given Ginger her other name. They had moved to Fort Worth, Texas, because of Rogers's work, and Lela's career burgeoned there. Not ony did she again get work as a reporter on the local paper, she also took to managing the Fort Worth symphony orchestra and writing pageants about the history of Texas – several of these naturally starred her now thirteen-year-old daughter.

Gentleman Jack: Edward Jackson Culpepper, the first of Ginger's dancing partners and the first of five husbands: they married when she was 17.

When Ginger was about eight, there had been the chance for her to audition for movies. Lela had rejected the idea on the grounds that her little girl needed a "proper upbringing", but now she was not so sure. Ginger was already showing promise as an athlete and a pianist, and in 1925, when Eddie Foy, the great vaudeville comic, came through Fort Worth with a show that needed a substitute dancer, Ginger was allowed, even encouraged, to audition and got the job.

From there it was but a short time-step to local talent shows and church concerts. While claiming that she didn't want her daughter to end up in show business, Lela became the theatrical mother from hell, urging her daughter onto the stage whenever possible.

Not that Ginger showed much sign of resistance; indeed, she couldn't wait to get her formal schooling out of the way and turn her athletic skills to dance marathons. In January 1926, while not yet fifteen, she was already appearing in the Dallas Charleston contests as part of a three-girl act billed as "Ginger and her Redheads".

First prize there, which they won, was a four-week touring engagement at a hundred dollars a week, and by the spring of that year Ginger was already on her first magazine cover – that of the *US Vaudeville News*. By now Lela seems to have decided that Ginger's rather than her own

> *While claiming that she still didn't really want her daughter to end up in show business, Lela seems to have become the theatrical mother from hell, urging her daughter onto the stage at every possible opportunity.*

career was the one to go for. With another marriage falling apart, she began to work for her daughter as manager, chaperone and gag-writer on the southern vaudeville circuit and continued for the next three years, taking twenty per cent of her income in return. Reviews were generally enthusiastic, praising "legs as fast as lightning" and "a sweet stage disposit-ion", convincing both mother and daughter that the wicked stage was to be their future. Lela, however, always maintained that she only really started to push Ginger once she saw that her daughter's own mind was made

Broadway to Hollywood: Ginger in 1930.

still some way from the top of the bill and still some way from a major theatre. Now, for the first time, Ginger decided to declare her teenage independence from Lela. She had first fallen for a show dancer called Jack Culpepper as a child when they were both living in Texas and he was an admirer of her aunt. He had also gone into the vaudeville business, and, after a lightning honeymoon, the two went on the road as Ginger and Pepper, a speciality dancing act, an endeavour that did nothing to assuage Lela's horror.

The partnership was a disaster on stage and off: she was seventeen, he twelve years older, and mother remained livid. "Don't you come back to me," she said, as Ginger recalled sixty years later, "one year from now dragging a baby to leave on my doorstep: you are headed for wonderful opportunities, but if you pursue this wedding you lose me forever."

Not so in fact. Within a year Jack had taken to the bottle, and Ginger had taken up a solo act and gone back to her mother who was now divorcing her own second husband. Theirs was perhaps the only one of the family relationships truly made in heaven.

Back on the road, Ginger joined Eddie Lowry and his band, went on to stooge for the comedian Willie Howard and ended up as a bandstand singer with the Paul Ash Orchestra, where for the first time in her career she really got lucky. Ash had a booking at the Paramount Theatre in Brooklyn, in between the movies, and this meant that at last Ginger was off the Southern and MidWest touring circuit and into the environs of New York, where there was not only considerable nightclub activity but also a thriving movie industry and, of course, Broadway itself. Suddenly it was possible for her to think of at least three potential careers.

up. "People say she had no childhood," Lela complained later to a Hollywood magazine, "well, neither did I. I started at sixteen as a reporter. Believe me, it's better that way."

It was not an easy time, playing deadbeat vaudeville in rural Texas towns known only to their residents. Sometimes mother had to join Ginger in the act, whereupon they would be billed as sisters; at other times Ginger would appear alone as a "disappointment act", meaning that someone fractionally better known had failed to turn up. At best, she would play the Paramount circuit, singing and dancing between the films in short musical revues; at worst, she would perform recitations about animals in a coy "baby voice" that she went on employing well into her movie career for apparently comic effect.

By 1928 they had reached New Orleans,

"I was nineteen years old, and starring on Broadway in a show by George and Ira Gershwin at a thousand dollars a week; top of the world Ma!"

Studio Siren: RKO begins to turn her into a cover girl, 1931.

New York was a new world for the little girl from Independence, Missouri. On Christmas Day 1929, only a few months after she had first reached Brooklybn as a bandstand singer for the `paramount, Ginger was already opening on Broadway, admittedly way below the title, in an undistinguished Kalmar-Ruby musical called *Top Speed*. She had gone along to the audition hoping for little more than a chorus part or a walk-on; what she ended up with was the second lead, and a lucky break worthy of one of the subplots in 42nd Street or the Stage Door, movies she was later to make in Hollywood. This Christmas, Ginger was really in luck. First of all, the show had a more than usually bland leading lady in Irene Delroy, who offered next to no competition

of any kind; secondly, Ginger had the flashy role of a wealthy heiress who has the courage to fall in love with a stockbroker's clerk; and thirdly, she got to lead the chorus in the one showstopper, "Hot and Bothered". Not entirely surprisingly, she therefore captured such good reviews as there were. The New York Times called her "an impudent young thing who carries her youth and humor to the point where they become completely charming", though the Herald-Tribune reckoned that she was "unlikely ever to disturb the Terpsichorean Hall of Fame". In other words, to rewrite a famous casting-card on her later partner, "acts a bit, not much of a singer, dances well and can do t he jokes".

Top Speed was just another so-so Broadway musical that came and went without much

With Norman Foster in *Young Man of Manhattan* **(1930), her first feature film, made in New York while she was still playing on Broadway.**

trace in the days when there were still regularly about fifty of them in any New York season; but its importance to Ginger was that for the first time she experienced theatrical legitimacy. With one first night, she was off the big-band and vaudeville circuit forever and not just into straight theatre either. With an energy that was always to be her hallmark, she went out with her mother to the Astoria Studios to look for daytime work in the

comic shorts - which were pouring out of there as rapidly as musicals were flooding down Broadway - as soon as she found herself safely installed on stage at night. At first, her screen prospects didn't look too good. A Paramount talent scout sent to have a look at her in *Top Speed* noted, "Just another Charleston dancer who can't act; but she's cute and plump and pretty, and might do all right in a flapper role".

Ginger was a quick-witted flapper with very few lines, but one of them just happened to be a classic: in a nightclub, she utters the immortal words "Cigarette me, Big Boy."

Paramount Paramour: Ginger in 1930, at the start of her long studio career in Hollywood.

What she, in fact, did all right in was a series of musical short-subjects with Rudy Vallee. She then did a walk-on in her first feature film, where once again her luck was in. The film was *Young Man of Manhattan* (1930), a newspaper story starring Claudette Colbert and Charley Ruggles. Ginger was a quick-witted flapper with very few lines, but one of them just happened to be a classic: finally meeting Ruggles in a nightclub, she utters the immortal words "Cigarette me, Big Boy."

And there was better to come. While still playing eight shows a week for *Top Speed* she shot two more features, *The Sap From*

Syracuse and *Queen High*, neither of which gave her anything very much to do but both of which added up to the Paramount notion that she might now be worth sending out to Hollywood on a studio contract. Ginger, urged on as ever by Lela, was just about to sign, when she was sharp enough to notice something else going on: a backstage rumour around Broadway that there was a new Gershwin musical going into rehearsal with a wondrous score and at least two roles capable of making stars. Ginger had just lost the chance of a *Ziegfeld Follies* with Al Jolson (because the star demanded his future wife, Ruby Keeler, get the part instead) and she

With Jack Oakie in *The Sap from Syracuse* (1930), her third feature film – "a competent ingenue, should soon become popular with the move folks on the coast" (*Motion Picture Herald*). In Britain, the picture was retitled *The Sap from Abroad.*

was still half-inclined to head out to Hollywood and a movie career. But one meeting with George Gershwin at his apartment was enough to convince her that such a move would be a mistake. He offered her the role of the lovelorn postmistress in *Girl Crazy* (or, as it is now known in revised form, *Crazy For You*) and, still more importantly, he began to play at his own piano the song he said he had written especially for her - the one that begins "They're writing songs of love, But not for me . . ."

In rehearsal things went from good to better: a young Broadway dancer called Fred Astaire was called in to choreograph one of her dance routines. Thus, a rehearsal afternoon on Broadway was the first time Fred and Ginger ever danced arm in arm, if not cheek to cheek. The classic, vintage score

also featured such numbers as "I Got Rhythm", "What Love Has Done To Me" and, for Ginger, "Embraceable You". As they opened, however, one little problem arose. Just as Ginger had stolen *Top Speed* from Irene Delroy, there was competition from another newcomer in the cast of *Girl Crazy*, the one who sang "I Got Rhythm", the one who got all the notices; she was Ethel Merman.

Merman's memoirs note somewhat acidly that "Ginger was pretty and could sing and dance, but nobody would ever call her 'The Voice': she sang charmingly, but her songs never required real power." Nevertheless, the show remained a happy one backstage, to such an extent that when *Girl Crazy* was filmed with Judy Garland in Rogers's original role, they even re-named the character "Ginger".

> *Socially, Ginger was a huge success. She was bright, bubbly, and, to put it politely, a party girl. Her upbringing in backwoods vaudeville, overlaid now with a patina of New York wit and urbanity picked up around the side streets of Broadway, made her a better guest than the more vapid Hollywood blondes.*

While they were co-starring in *Girl Crazy* on Broadway by night - for all of 270 performances - Ginger and Ethel were also filming by day in Paramount's *Follow the Leader*, where roles were somewhat reversed as Rogers played the understudy becoming a star in Merman's place when big Ethel gets kidnapped. After that came an all-star newspaper drama directed by Dorothy Arzner, *Honor Among Lovers*, where Ginger found herself way down an unusually starry cast list headed by Claudette Colbert, Fredric March, Pat O'Brien and Ralph Morgan. But now, pleading her daughter's exhaustion with the stage and screen life, Lela managed to get Ginger out of her Paramount contract.

Exhaustion was not the only reason. Looking carefully down the studio rosters, Lela had concluded that whereas Paramount would always be inclined to cast her girl as a dizzy blonde, Pathé might offer her more intriguing work. "I think I may come to regret this release," said Lasky of Paramount, in one of those prescient quotes that might have been designed for movie-star memoirs.

Certainly nothing Ginger first did at Pathé, except her decision to join the studio in Hollywood, justified Lasky's regret or suggested she had made a wise career move. She and Lela travelled west as soon as *Girl Crazy* closed, and Pathé (at that time a quota-quickie studio) rapidly put her into a succession of B-to-Z features. There was *The Tip-Off* (Ginger as Baby Face, the prizefighter's moll); *Suicide Fleet* (Ginger as the girl the sailors left on shore); and *Carnival Boat* (Ginger as the sassy showboat entertainer falling for William Boyd, before he fell for Hopalong Cassidy).

At this juncture both Pathé and Ginger agreed that they had made a horrendous mistake, and her studio option was abruptly dropped; but, having only just made the move to California, she decided to stay and survive the freelance life rather than make a sheepish return to Broadway.

Socially, Ginger was a huge success. She was bright, bubbly, and, to put it politely, a party girl. Her upbringing in backwoods vaudeville, overlaid now with a patina of New York wit and urbanity picked up around the side streets of Broadway, made her an altogether better guest then the more vapid Hollywood blondes. She was also undeniably multi-talented. She may not have been a great actress, singer, dancer or comedienne, but she could get by well enough in all four capacities at a time of the very early Thirties when most Hollywood stars were still learning how to speak and walk simultaneously on screen.

Like Katharine Hepburn, who was to

Before Blonde: Ginger in an early Pathé one-reel comedy.

follow her out west from Broadway in a year or two, Ginger, though without much of her edgy, nervous energy, brought a welcome air of another America to Southern California. In a reversal of the *Girl Crazy* plot, she was the small-town girl from the back of beyond come to show them a thing or two about survival in the big movie city.

Accordingly, once the Pathé contract collapsed, Ginger simply did whatever came down the pike. In her first full year in Hollywood she made a total of seven pictures - none of them remotely memorable and all of them for different studios. At First National she did *The Tenderfoot*, another backstage story, based on a George Kaufman

play, combining what appeared to be her two major assets: the ability to be a comic foil to the star (in this case, Joe E. Brown), and the talent she had for looking utterly at home in a dressing-room, surrounded by other aspiring stars.

Then she went to Monogram for a minor thriller called *The Thirteenth Guest*, to Fox for *Hat-Check Girl*, in which she played a caretaker of the coathangers opposite Ben Lyon, another rising comedian ("smooth, spicy and sassy" thought *Variety*). She then went back to First National, because Joe E. Brown had asked for her again, for a mistaken-identity farce called *You Said A Mouthful* and this time *Photoplay* noted that

"Miss Rogers was positively made for a bathing suit."

None of this could, by any stretch of the imagination, be considered high art, and Ginger's own reservations were characteristically evident in one of her early Hollywood interviews: "I don't know whether I like the stage or screen best. I do love the applause of an audience: but then again, pictures are so fascinating - you reach many millions through them, and you make more money, too."

Not that she had altogether given up the stage. When her movie career was resolutely failing to lift off, she joined Eddie Dowling and Ray Dooley in a stage act called "Brevities" which allowed her to parody Ethel Merman in her *Girl Crazy* role and to do eccentric impressions of Chevalier and Jolson. It was as though she could still not quite break the backstage connection, and happily her first good film in Hollywood was about just that predicament.

Early in her Hollywood life Ginger had struck up a close friendship with Mervyn LeRoy, who took a more than professional interest in her choice of movies. Therefore, when Joan Blondell dropped out of a new musical, one for which Ginger had already unsuccessfully auditioned, it was LeRoy who urged her to take on what seemed a thoroughly unrewarding role. The picture was yet another backstage chorus-girl saga, this time starring Dick Powell and Ruby Keeler, relative newcomers, a fact that did not ease Ginger's sense of yet again being passed over for the best roles.

Anytime Annie was on her way to the big time, and she was still only a year past her twenty-first birthday.

Once more, however, she was cast in the kind of role she seemed to play best. Anytime Annie (so called because "the only time she said no was when she didn't hear the question," as another character in the script says) was a cane-carrying, fast-talking chorus girl who recommends Keeler to step into the role vacated by an ailing Bebe Daniels. Keeler goes out on stage an understudy and comes back a star. The film was, of course, *42nd Street*, one that established several careers, not least that of the mercurial, epic choreographer Busby Berkeley.

Ginger only got to sing a few choruses of *Shuffle Off To Buffalo* with Una Merkel, but they were enough. That classic Al Dubin-Harry Warren score, with its great anthems to Broadway and laments for the Depression and its cynicism ("When she knows as much as we know," chant Rogers and Merkel, "She'll be on her way to Reno") kick-started her film-musical career. Anytime Annie was on her way to the big time, and she was still only a year past her twenty-first birthday.

RKO now offered her what they ruthlessly described as a "non-starring contract" and Ginger, true to her form as the girl who never said no, took it, only to end up in the dire *Professional Sweetheart*, one of those pictures with which Hollywood (as it would do twenty years later when television became the enemy) tried to destroy the new threat of radio by making laborious fun of it on screen. Ginger's voice was frequently thought not to be up to the songs, and she was dubbed, for the only time in her career, by the black singer Ella Motten.

CHAPTER THREE

"Did you ever see a dream walking?"

*I*t was Arlene Croce, the definitive dance historian of the Astaire-Rogers movies, who best summarised Ginger's career prospects in these months before the two found each other on screen: "She was a Clara Bow type, but by then the type was fading fast; when the Bow image faded into the Jean Harlow one, Rogers went blonde and quickly made the transition from Twenties flapper to Thirties gold-digger . . . by early 1933 she had found her form temporarily in the kind of parts that Joan Blondell and Glenda Farrell were also playing, but this time, instead of losing herself in the type, she wiggled around in it trying to make it fit her. There had always been a strong element of precocity in her personality, something startlingly out of tune with her cutie face and figure. Astaire, when he came into the movies, was already formed as an artist and a personality, but

movie audiences watched Ginger Rogers grow up. The bratty, imitative cleverness that was so large a part of her talent sometimes got in her way, and she desperately needed polishing. In some of her early movies she even suggested a kind of junior Mae West, but without Mae's all-consuming self-knowledge and control. Ginger was a hot mama at the age of twenty-two. It was better than being a simple, straight ingenue, but it was a rotten fate for a clever child. Astaire would turn her into a goddess."

But not just yet. First she had to do a penny-dreadful thriller called *A Shriek in the Night* and yet another showgirl musical, this one supporting Joan Blondell as a character called suitably enough Flip in *Broadway Bad*. There was better to come. Her success in *42nd Street*, and the ongoing alliance with Mervyn LeRoy then got her into *Gold Diggers of 1933*, reuniting her with the composers Al

Ginger and Fred: to songs from America's greatest 1930s composers, they danced duets that remain sixty years later the untouchable standard for screen dancing. For the first and only time on camera, a profound partnership was created by the act of dancing only.

ABOVE "I want to sin and suffer – and all I do is suffer": Ginger's first film at RKO was the 1933 *Professional Sweetheart*, though previous working titles had been *The Purity Girl* and *Careless*. "Cute and clever" thought *The New York Times*: "Miss Rogers has rarely been more entertaining."

RIHGT The second of her five husbands, the actor Lew Ayres, on their wedding day in 1934.

Dubin and Harry Warren, the choreographer Busby Berkeley and the stars Ruby Keeler and Dick Powell. She still only achieved ninth billing, but this time she opened the picture in a dress made entirely of silver dollars, singing her own pig-Latin version of "We're in the Money"; as showcases go, there have been considerably more opaque ones. Her only other major number, for which she was dressed in black sequins and perched atop a white piano, was cut unfortunately when the picture went way over length to accommodate the lavish Berkeley dance numbers. But "We're in the Money" would do nicely and things were looking up in Ginger's private life too. With the LeRoy liaison unlikely to lead to much else on screen or off, she had now met up with a young actor called Lew Ayres, of *All Quiet on the Western Front*, and soon they were making a picture together - a comedy drama set on a racetrack and called predictably *Don't Bet on Love*. They were "a rather goodlooking couple", said the *Los Angeles Times*, whereupon they announced their engagement, which was followed by a wedding that brought Lela considerably less distress than Ginger's first.

That marriage survived in theory until 1940, but in practice for only a couple of years or so (Ginger later blamed Lew's "love of late-night parties" and his insistence on a prenuptial contract several decades before these became truly fashionable). She continued on the film front and went back to Paramount to sing "Did You Ever See A Dream Walking?" in *Sitting Pretty*. This was the eighth film she had made in the past twelve months, and the thirteenth since arriving in Hollywood barely three years

earlier. No wonder her mother was now hailing her as "the greatest little picture-saver in the business".

But Lela had always been astute enough to realise, as had Ginger, that the life of a jobbing freelance picture-saver was not really the one she had come out west to do. She had to get a studio to sign her long-term and then to come up with some sort of a career plan.

Once again luck was with them when it was most needed: RKO was having yet another rethink of its roster of studio contract players and decided they could, after all, offer Ginger seven years. Moreover, they already had another musical lined up for her, and maybe even a partner. Her old dancing

Ginger *Sitting Pretty* with Jack Oakie in 1933: "always one of the pleasures of the cinema, a girl who combines looks, grace and an unaffected wit" (*New York Herald Tribune*). And in this case a head for heights – the director (left) is Harry Joe Brown.

With Jack Haley in *Sitting Pretty* (1933): Ginger was the waitress and he was the songwriter on their way to Hollywood fame and fortune.

master from *Girl Crazy*, Fred Astaire, had by now decided to follow Ginger to Hollywood since his sister Adele had opted for marriage and a stage retirement, leaving him all too alone on Broadway.

He was very soon given an RKO contract as well, and the studio decided that both Fred and Ginger could now be usefully slotted into a vehicle designed for Dolores del Rio and Joel McCrea. In the event McCrea dropped out, to be replaced by Gene Raymond, while the singer Raul Roulien also had to be accommodated. Thus it was that

Astaire and Rogers made their screen-partnership debut with fifth and fourth billing respectively, Ginger just getting the edge in respect of her greater screen experience.

In no sense was *Flying Down To Rio* a picture actually designed for their individual or joint talents, but as the *Herald-Tribune* duly noted, "the inspired music of Vincent Youmans, the grace of Fred Astaire, the dark beauty of Dolores del Rio, the singing of Raoul Roulien, the comedy of Ginger Rogers and the love-making of Gene Raymond

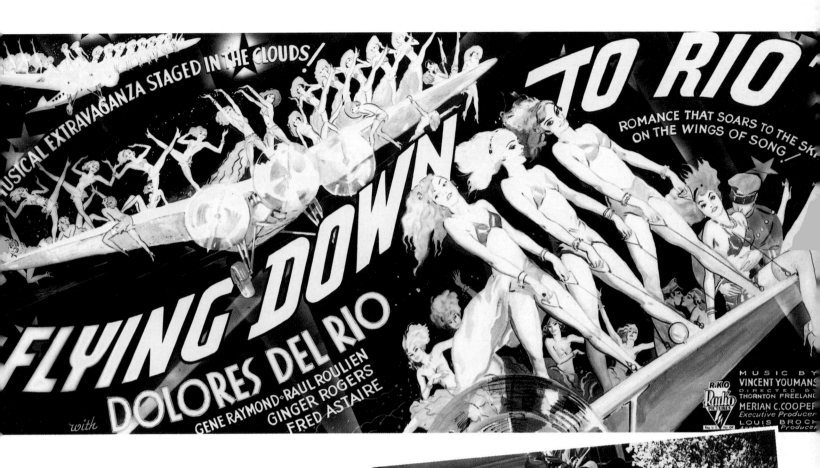

ABOVE The first with Fred: *Flying Down to Rio* (1933) was Ginger's twentieth film and the one where she danced the Carioca head to head with Astaire at the start of their ten-film, sixteen-year partnership.

RIGHT On the set of *Flying Down to Rio*: "one glorious Hollywood holiday" in the view of the *New York American*.

combine to make this a glorious Hollywood holiday."

Ginger sang the title song, leading a team of gold-dressed maidens strapped to the wings of aeroplanes hovering over a South American resort hotel. She also sang "Music Makes Me". But she and Fred only really danced together once in the whole picture, and it was a routine that the perfectionist Astaire always thought they had under-rehearsed. Nevertheless, if Fred and Ginger could be said to be born anywhere, it was in that "Carioca", a rhythmic rhumba they danced with their heads pressed together.

It wasn't until filming began that Cooper realised he had stumbled onto something special ... Thus, out of their almost accidental teaming for 'Rio', was born the greatest double asset the Hollywood musical was ever to enjoy.

ABOVE "The grace of Fred Astaire, the comedy of Ginger Rogers . . .": *Flying Down to Rio* (1933).

LEFT *The Carioca*: "Two heads together, that's how the dance is begun".

Hardly any review of the movie failed to mention the sequence, and even during the shooting it was clear that a star duet had suddenly appeared almost out of nowhere. The producer, Merian C. Cooper, had originally cast Dorothy Jordan in Ginger's role, but he then decided to marry her instead. It wasn't until filming began that Cooper realised he had stumbled onto something so special that it would even be worth bringing in the *New Yorker* wit Robert Benchley to boost Astaire's still-negligible dialogue.

Thus, out of their almost accidental teaming for *Rio*, was born the greatest double asset the Hollywood musical was ever to enjoy. Off the set, the Rogers and Astaire friendship was cool at best. As Ginger later noted. "Fred and I had the great privilege of working together in ten films; magical as they were, my movie career included a total sixty-three others."

Fred was also always eager to disprove the notion that they were bound together for a working life. His sister Adele had always been his favourite dancing partner, and he said of *Rio*, "I knew I hadn't yet scratched the surface of any real dancing on screen." All the same, film distributors and critics and audiences began urging RKO to get them back together

Twenty Million Sweethearts
(1934): this time Dick Powell was
the singing waiter, Ginger was the
actress who cured his terror of
radio broadcasts. An earlier title,
Hot Air, was abandoned for
obvious reasons.

again as soon as possible. The studio had in
fact already paved the way for a return
engagement by making sure that the last shot
in the picture went to Fred and Ginger,
rather than the ostensible stars Dolores del
Rio and Gene Raymond. The problem was
that nobody had any immediate idea of a
script that could follow up their sudden
"Carioca" triumph.

Astaire indeed left Hollywood altogether,
because he had already agreed to play Cole
Porter's *The Gay Divorce* on Broadway and in
London. Ginger, now at least able to relax in
the knowledge that her future casting was

RKO's problem rather than hers, was
assigned to six more non-Astaire pictures in
her usual quick succession.

Though she was generally now in much
larger roles, none of these pictures even
attempted to capitalise on her new-found
fame as a dancer: *Chance at Heaven* was a
romantic comedy with Joel McCrea; *Rafter
Romance* had "barely the energy to make it to
the back half of a double feature" (*Variety*);
Finishing School had her as Frances Dee's best
friend; *Twenty Million Sweethearts* allowed her
to sing, with Dick Powell, a Dubin-Warren
score infinitely less distinguished than the

two of theirs she had already filmed; *Change of Heart* cast her supporting Janet Gaynor; and *Upperworld* had her back as a hard-boiled showgirl. It was as though she had never flown down to Rio at all.

But then, at the end of 1933, Fred came back to her, this time with *The Gay Divorce*, in which he had already triumphed on stage. Its title immediately had to be changed to *The Gay Divorcée* to avoid offending current audience susceptibilities (the problem was the divorce, not at that time the "gay"), and only one of Porter's original stage songs was retained - happily for all concerned it was "Night and Day".

The rest of the score, cobbled together by such local Hollywood talent as Mack Gordon, Harry Revel and Con Conrad, was a hotchpotch, though it did include "Needle in a Haystack" for Fred, and their second great dance routine, "The Continental," which ran all of twenty-two minutes, a length for a screen musical number hitherto undreamed, even by Busby Berkeley.

The plot here was minimal. (Astaire is mistaken for a professional co-respondent, hired so that Rogers can get her divorce), but it still required three writers plus two dance directors, though as already usual, Astaire took care of his own routines with the help of Hermes Pan.

"The Continental" won the first Academy Award ever given to a song, and by the time the rushes were shown, RKO knew they

> *"The Continental" won the first Academy Award ever given to a song, and by the time the rushes were shown, RKO knew they simply had to keep the dancers together in a succession of similar plots.*

simply had to keep the dancers together in a succession of similar plots. *Roberta* was even announced during the shooting, and the guidelines for writers were now clear: Fred was nearly always to be the professional dancer who has to convince the somewhat better-born Ginger that he is a suitable escort on the dance floor and partner in marriage. They dance, they flirt, they fight, they dance some more, they get married. What they almost never do, curiously enough, is kiss each other.

Aside from "The Continental", itself a huge production number, Astaire and Rogers only actually dance for about ten minutes of *The Gay Divorcée*, but thanks to what Noel Coward was once to call "the potency of cheap music" our false impression is that they are locked in each others arms throughout the picture.

"Chance is the fool's name for fate," as they say in *The Gay Divorcée* and chance, first in the form of the "Carioca" and now "The Continental", had thrown them together forever in film history. But no sooner was the film complete, and Fred already starting to plan with Pan the dance routines for Jerome Kern's *Roberta* than Ginger, ever eager to prove that she had a career away from Astaire, began filming *Romance in Manhattan* as, guess what? - a hard-boiled chorus girl falling in love with Francis Lederer, an impoverished immigrant cabdriver. If Ginger was terrified of being typecast as Fred's dancing partner, how curious that her roles away from him led to even greater restrictions of character.

CHAPTER FOUR

"To breathe an atmosphere that simply reeks of class"

In the view of many movie-musical historians, not least John Mueller, it was within their third picture, Jerome Kern's *Roberta* (1935), that Fred and Ginger as a screen partnership finally took off into the stratosphere. "Only in *Roberta*" Mueller wrote, "do the two performers seem comfortable enough and confident enough fully to achieve the spirited gaiety, the irrepressible charm and the emotional depth that became the trademarks of their collaboration: it is in *Roberta* that Astaire and Rogers transcend partnership and become co-conspirators.

Yet, here again, memory tends to be at fault. The central romantic partnership of *Roberta* is not that of Astaire and Rogers at all, but of Irene Dunne and a wildly ill-at-ease Randolph Scott, who seems somehow to have mislaid his horse. Astaire and Rogers are in there essentially for dancing and comic relief. But by now RKO was so sure of the team's stardom that it had all their numbers end with a kind of pause during which a cinema audience could, and indeed did,

applaud their work, even though it was still Dunne who got top billing.

Remade seventeen years later as *Lovely To Look At* (with Marge and Gower Champion in the Astaire-Rogers roles), *Roberta* was essentially a fashion parade, and the only way to give Fred enough to do was to combine two roles played on Broadway two years before by Bob Hope and George Murphy. About a third of that original score survived, but it was enough. A picture that included "Smoke Gets In Your Eyes", "I Won't Dance" and "Let's Begin" (all as dances for Fred and Ginger), as well as "Hard to Handle", could not be accused of failing to deliver on the pair's previous promise. The posters said it all: "Kern's dazzling stage success is ten times more tantalising on screen . . . a heartload of romance in Paris at lovetime . . . a lifetime of laughter, a world of joy, a riot of rhythm and a screenful of dancing". If the screenwriting wasn't always wonderful in Astaire-Rogers vehicles, at least the poster-writing was reliable in its extremities.

Fred noted, in his usually clenched way, "*Roberta* was fun: I tackled it with a bit more

"Never Gonna Dance": from *Swing Time* (1936): "in the film, this is the end of their affair; in real life, it is the end of Astaire and Rogers's golden age. Fred's monogamous instinct is to quit dancing if he can't dance with her". (Arlene Croce).

confidence and enthusiasm than usual . . . we were going through the sort of show business dream-sequence where you can't do anything wrong professionally: it was a winning groove, and Ginger and I never failed to find plenty to laugh about."

For her, the memories were of:

"Fred, along with Hermes Pan, spending days putting the steps together; generally speaking, we practiced our dance numbers for eight hours a day for six weeks prior to principal photography. But because I was always working on other pictures as well, I was frequently unavailable and in those instances Hermes would step in and dance my part with Fred. When I arrived, they would then teach me the routines but Hermes played 'Ginger' often enough for

some waggish writers to call him 'Fred's favourite dancing partner'."

Whether Ginger ever was, remained a matter for some debate. But on screen they achieved the illusion in dance after dance so powerfully as to allay the fears that Fred was still expressing, as late as the making of *Roberta* in letters to his agent:

"*What* is all this talk about me being teamed with Ginger Rogers? I will not have it - I did not go into pictures to be teamed with her or anyone else, and if that is the program in mind for me I will not stand for it. I don't mind making another picture with her, but the team idea is out. I've just managed to live down one partnership and I don't want to be bothered with any more. I'd rather not make any more pictures for RKO if I have to be

Least known of all the Astaire-Rogers classics, *Roberta* (1935) was a Broadway hit for Jerome Kern "but it's most pleasant moments" thought *Time* magazine, "occur when Fred and Ginger turn the story upside down and dance on it like gay elves on a sunbeam."

teamed up with one of these movie 'queens' . . . Please understand that I'm just against the idea, and if I am ever to get anywhere on screen it will be as one not as two."

Happily Astaire's then agent, Leland Hayward, was astute enough to talk him out of walking away from the greatest success that he or Ginger were ever to enjoy. *Roberta* led straight on to *Top Hat* for him, though as usual Ginger had nipped off elsewhere to play opposite William Powell in a high society comedy-thriller called *Star of Midnight*, for which all she got were reviews pointing out that she badly lacked the nonchalant wit of Powell's usual *Thin Man* partner Myrna Loy.

But then it was back to the bandstand and to what many reckon the best of all the Astaire-Rogers musicals. *Top Hat* was the first

in which they received top billing, and the first to have an integral score by Irving Berlin. And it was not just any old Berlin score; including "No Strings", "Cheek to Cheek", "Isn't This A Lovely Day?" and of course "The Piccolino" which gave the picture its now-ritual all-dancing big finish. Again the plot was a simple matter of mistaken identity and mattered not a jot: by now, as in the old P. G. Wodehouse or Aldwych farce tradition, a semi-permanent repertory company of recognisable screen types (Edward Everett Horton, the ineffable butler Eric Blore and Helen Broderick) had built up around the central duo. Their own irritability would frequently centre on Ginger's choice of dress, often one with feathers that would get up Fred's nose in

Ginger with the composer Irving Berlin on the set of *Top Hat* (1935).

OPPOSITE The feathers that caused all the fuss: Ginger and Fred in *Top Hat*'s "Cheek to Cheek" routine (1935).

more ways than one. You had to stay on the set, said one costume designer, until the first shot of her in any new gown was safely in the can; otherwise you'd come back and find she'd added little bows and flashing jewels all over it just to make sure she'd be noticed by the camera.

Ginger, for her part, had the grace not to laugh too loudly when not only Fred's top hat but also his cherished toupee fell into the Lido canal that had been recreated on set, but relations one way and another were still somewhat strained. From time to time one of the more theatre-oriented critics would suggest that Fred might be better partnered by Gertrude Lawrence or Jessie Matthews, while for Ginger herself the career plan was still to end up as Carole Lombard or Katharine Hepburn rather than just the girl who danced with Fred.

Given such tensions, it's a miracle the movies looked so carefree. It was a constant source of irritation to Ginger that,

considering how many films she had made compared to him, she was second-billed, and she resented the teams of choreographers and dance advisers within whom Fred walled himself on the set while creating his most elaborate routines. Nor was she exactly delighted to learn that, when Fred eventually agreed to sign a seven-year, seven-picture contract, it was specified therein that he would only have to make half his pictures with her, unless he chose otherwise.

Wisely, while she went off, after *Top Hat*, to make her first solo starring vehicle, *In Person*, which was about an agoraphobic film star wanting to be alone with George Brent, Astaire began to think about their next partnership, utterly unperturbed by what Arlene Croce came to notice as the curious time-warp in which their films were already locked:

"In the class-conscious Thirties, it was possible to imagine characters who spent their entire lives in evening dress, to imagine

The best roles they ever had, and the most triumphant: on a budget of $600,000, *Top Hat* grossed $3 million.

Top Hat took in three million dollars at the box office on its initial release in 1935, and by the end of the decade had become the second-highest-grossing film of all time. Garson Kanin, who would later direct Ginger in *Bachelor Mother,* noted, "Never before and never since have I seen an audience stand up and cheer like that at the end of a picture: I sat through it twice and that evening took my brother, who also wanted to see it twice; so I

> *By now Ginger was always known to Fred as "Feathers" because of the ones that had caused him so much trouble during "Cheek to Cheek".*

saw it four times that day, and the next morning I was back in the queue to see it again."

By now Ginger was always known to Fred as "Feathers" because of the ones that had caused him so much trouble during "Cheek to Cheek", and in their next picture it was to be the beads that got him, beads sewn to her sleeve which she would whip painfully across his face during the "Let's Face the Music and Dance" sequence of *Follow the Fleet.*

Already separated from Lew Ayres, Ginger was being seen around town with James Stewart and the billionaires Howard Hughes and Alfred Vanderbilt. Her energy on screen also remained undiminished: for *Follow the Fleet* she danced "Let Yourself Go", "Let's Face the Music and Dance" and "I'm Putting All My Eggs in One Basket". But this was the film in which Fred and Ginger bade farewell to the 1920s and moved into the era of swing, even reversing their usual roles so that

them as faintly preposterous holdovers from the Twenties, slipping from their satin beds at twilight, dancing the night away and then stumbling, top-hatted and ermine-tangled, out of speakeasies at dawn: it was a dead image, a faded cartoon of the pre-Crash, pre-Roosevelt Prohibition era, but it was the only image of luxury that people believed in and *Top Hat* revived it as a corrected vision of elegance . . . this is a Thirties romance of the Twenties, the sins of the decade wiped clean by a flow of lyrical optimism, all innocence regained in the exhilaration of 'stepping out, my dear, to breathe an atmosphere that simply reeks of class'.

Ginger and her men: *In Person* (1935) was her first solo starring picture – songs by Oscar Levant and Dorothy Fields, dances by Hermes Pan.

they went distinctly downmarket, with Astaire as a gum-chewing sailor and Rogers a dance-hall hostess. This picture was plot-heavy, with no real attempt to integrate the dance numbers, so that "Let's Face the Music and Dance" almost stands as a short movie of its own. But now the partnership was really all that mattered. Having first caught public attention, as John Kobal once noted, "as two vulnerable sophisticates who meet and, after a cautious start, acknowledge their love in a succession of dances for which the world is their ballroom", they were now taking tentative steps towards modernity. Their only true duo-rivals on stage were, perhaps, Noel and Gertie, and on screen William Powell and Myrna Loy - but none of them ever danced a step on screen together, or got an

invitation through the mail.

It was Kobal who also identified what separated Ginger from any of Fred's subsequent dancing partners:

"She could follow him exactly, dancing almost like his shadow rather than his prima ballerina. She was a clever faker: when she danced with Astaire, one looked at her face for reactions instead of her feet. Besides which she was pert, pretty and had an appealing, vulnerable quality which she would disguise behind a facade of caustic repartee . . . Other partners brought out the romantic, the classical and the technical aspects of the man, but Ginger was, at the end of the day, the affectionate look back at a life shared, a past remembered and the value of lasting: in short, the rewards that come to

ABOVE Fred and Ginger's fifth dance partnership was later remade as *Hit The Deck*. The score had seven new songs by Irving Berlin, most of which Ginger danced. In the view of *Variety*, "She now goes beyond the role of dancing *vis-à-vis* for Astaire and emerges as a corking stepper in her own right."

RIGHT *Swing Time*: sixth of the Astaires (1936), with a score by Jerome Kern and Dorothy Fields. "Miss Rogers shares 50-50 with Astaire and there will be those who give her an even greater share for her dancing and comic flair: she's finally gotten to the point where she dances as casually as her partner" (*The New York Times*).

two people who know from the outset that they will know each other always, warts and all, and whom living together has made into one."

Or, as Fred himself put it in "A Fine Romance", she was his strong, aged-in-the-wood woman. He himself had now danced his body so thin that you could practically spit through it, so theirs was not always the sexiest of screen partnerships. For that you had to look, later, toward Fred with Rita Hayworth. But, like his West End friends Noel Coward and Jack Buchanan, Astaire always had in his public presence a kind of elfin asexuality, utterly non-threatening to women and therefore infinitely attractive. It was left to Gene Kelly to bring a sense of butch danger to Hollywood dance routines.

Watching Fred dance is to understand how Puck or Ariel might have soft-shoe shuffled.

Ginger was earth to his air, which explained both the tenacity and the tensions of the alliance, though it was one about which some critics still had their doubts, not least Graham Greene:

"It needs an effort of mind, [he wrote of *Follow The Fleet*] to remember that Mr Fred Astaire was not invented by a film director, nor drawn by a film draughtsman: he is the nearest we are ever likely to get to a human Mickey Mouse: a touch of pathos, the sense of a courageous and impromptu intelligence, a capacity for getting into awkward situations: but Ginger Rogers will never quite attain Minnie's significance, for she is too brazen and self-sufficing and never matches his freedom, lightness or happiness."

For all that, *Follow the Fleet* (in which Tony Martin, Betty Grable and Lucille Ball can also fleetingly be glimpsed) was another marathon hit for Astaire and Rogers, their fifth in rapid succession. Even Ginger was now so confident of the partnership that she had given up going off to other pictures in between these musicals, and thus both of them were able to move straight on to rehearsals for *Swing Time,* with George Stevens replacing Mark Sandrich as their director, and a score by Jerome Kern and Dorothy Fields which was to include such classics as "The Way You Look Tonight", "A Fine Romance", "Bojangles of Harlem" and "Pick Yourself Up".

This time, in a certain echo of *Top Hat* (alternate Astaire-Rogers movies can usually be reckoned to have been built on the backs of the last one), Fred was a dandy of the Depression and Ginger was caught washing that man right out of her hair. Early titles had included "I Won't Dance" and "Never

Gonna Dance", and this of course is the movie in which Fred deliberately claims he can't dance in order to be taught by Ginger, and in which they're caught dancing in the snow instead of the rain. Otherwise, not much change. As Arlene Croce noted, "if you put *Top Hat* in a glass ball like a paperweight and turned it upside down, it would be *Swing Time.*"

As if aware that the duo really belonged in the decade just preceding the one in which they were living, RKO made sure that *Swing Time* was another nostalgia trip into the nightclubs and bars of 1920s Manhattan. By now Lela, always on set to ensure that her Ginger didn't get upscreened by whatever Fred and his faithful choreographer Hermes Pan had devised, had become so irritating to the Astaire team that she was given an entirely new job at the studio as head of the RKO talent school, where, to her credit, she discovered both Lucille Ball and Tyrone Power.

And there were those, even beyond herself and her mother, who believed Ginger deserved something better than to be forever Fred's dancing partner. Garson Kanin had tried to get the studio to give her *Mary of Scotland,* and even around the Astaire set there was a determination to try something different whenever possible. Thus *Swing Time* is full of odd reversals: it's Ginger, for once, who gets to open "A Fine Romance", Fred who pretends he can't dance, Ginger who is covered in shampoo for "The Way You Look Tonight". Even so, something terrible happened when *Swing Time* reached cinemas around the United States - audiences didn't.

> *And there were those even beyond herself who believed Ginger deserved something better than to be forever Fred's dancing partner.*

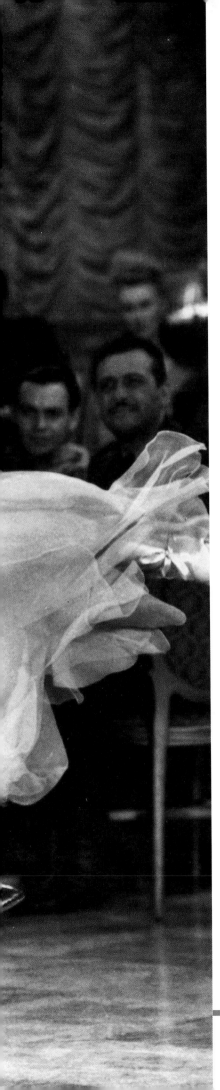

CHAPTER FIVE

"Let's call the whole thing off"

The picture opened well enough around Broadway and Sunset Boulevard, despite a rather sniffy review in the New York Times ("Neither good Kern nor good swing"). But what worried RKO for the first time were the box-office figures from the Midwest and the deep South. Suddenly Astaire and Rogers were not so hot and it was even rumoured that their next collaboration, the 1937 Shall We Dance?, would, in fact, be their last. The new film would have the first Gershwin screen score in seven years - George and Ira, coming off Porgy & Bess, were desperate to prove that they still had commercial credibility as well as operatic intentions - and the plot would feature Fred as an American ballet star who, dancing under a Russian name, falls in love not only with Ginger as a successful ballroom dancer but with her style of dancing as well.

The Gershwins' score included "They All Laughed", "They Can't Take That Away From Me" and the by now ritual "quarrel number", which in this case was "Let's Call the Whole Thing Off". The Gershwins themselves later declared they were less than happy with the way their numbers were treated in the film as a whole. This was only their second picture, and they were not as yet fully acclimatised to the differences between a Broadway number and a Hollywood one.

In all other respects, though, this was a joyous reunion for both Fred and Ginger with the Gershwins for whom both had worked on Broadway in the 1920s. As if to acknowledge that this, their seventh picture in less than five years, could be their last, each even got to dance with other partners - Ginger with Pete Theodore and Fred with the former Ziegfeld girl Harriet Hoctor.

Here, too, was "Slap that Bass", the number in which Fred first imitates and then dances to all the sounds of the ship's engine room, the kind of "speciality" number he most enjoyed, while "Let's Call the Whole Thing Off" was danced on roller skates. It seemed that, before they changed partners and danced elsewhere, Fred and Ginger wanted at least subconsciously to prove that nobody was ever going to be able to do it better.

Their last pre-war dance: *The Story of Vernon and Irene Castle* (1939): "What most Americans had done for recreation, Astaire and Rogers did with the insuferable dedication of the lifelong professional". (Arlene Croce)

RIGHT Trouble on the telephone: the film first called *Stepping Toes* became *Shall We Dance* (1937).

BELOW This was what they can't take away from us: Fred and Ginger in *Shall We Dance* (1937).

Both had long expressed their eagerness to work with others and now, with their box office returns falling fast, RKO decided to let them. Fred worked on *A Damsel in Distress* with the nineteen-year-old Joan Fontaine, while Ginger, who had been terrified of being "all washed up at thirty" (though that birthday was still four years away), was teamed with another RKO rebel, Katharine Hepburn, only recently declared "box-office poison".

Together, Hepburn and Rogers made *Stage Door*, the story of the ambitions, dreams and disappointments of life in a boarding-house entirely occupied by hopeful young actresses. This was another kind of team effort featuring not only Hepburn and Rogers but Adolphe Menjou, Lucille Ball, Constance Collier, Eve Arden,

Ann Miller and the newcomer Andrea Leeds who took home the only Oscar nomination.

To anyone who knew anything of the reality of Hepburn's early Broadway career, *Stage Door* was a joyous succession of backstage in-jokes. Menjou even modelled his performance on the demon director Jed Harris, and the play they are seen rehearsing is a thinly veiled parody of Kate's *The Lake,* with its famous line about the calla lilies being in bloom again. As for Ginger, the *New York Herald-Tribune* gave her the review she had been dreaming of all her career:

"It is Miss Rogers who gives the finest performance in this photoplay . . . for several years there has been a curious tendency on

ABOVE & LEFT The best of her non-Astaire Thirties movies: with Adolphe Menjou and Katharine Hepburn in *Stage Door* (1937).

RIGHT Eye to eye with James Stewart for *Vivacious Lady* (1938).

the part of people who should know better to suggest that she was merely a good-looking dancing girl who was lucky enough to have Fred Astaire for a partner. As a matter of fact, of course, she was a most important contributor to the success of the team and has always had an authentic and original talent as a light comedienne . . . now she proves conclusively that her gift for comedy is deft and delightful . . . in a scene in Adolphe Menjou's penthouse she succeeds in making the girl seem both alcoholic and entirely charming, and that is nothing short of an epic feat."

The hard-boiled showgirl was of course a role that Ginger had played many times before, but it was only on this occasion that the critics sat up and took notice. "When you think of Miss Rogers's former song and dance appearances", wrote Otis Fergusson, "it seems as though this is the first chance she has had to be something more than a camera object, and stand forth in her own right, pert and charming and just plain nice."

Morrie Ryskind's script (from an Edna Ferber-George Kaufman play) was considerably funnier than the recent Astaire screenplays, not least for the moment when Hepburn moves into Rogers' room with a mountain of luggage: "Let's just sleep in the hall," says Ginger, "no sense in crowding the trunks."

From there Ginger went on to play the nightclub singer whom James Stewart has to smuggle home to his disapproving parents in *Vivacious Lady* (directed by George Stevens, with whom she was now romantically entangled), and after that came *Having Wonderful Time*, which had her uneventfully romancing Douglas Fairbanks (junior) in summer camp.

It was then 1938, and time to get back to Fred. The break in their dance routine had given everyone time to rethink the partnership, and it was now felt audiences would like a greater concentration on story and character, with the dances emerging genuinely from the action instead of being

ABOVE "Both Miss Rogers and Mr Fairbanks have their followings, although neither will add to them through this picture" (*Variety*): *Having Wonderful Time* (1938).

TOP With Ralph Bellamy and Fred, off the set of *Carefree*, (1938).

virtually self-contained sequences. *Carefree* is the shortest of all their pictures (at just under ninety minutes) and the one that gives the greater emphasis to Ginger. Irving Berlin's score was mainly notable for "Change Partners", and this time a contemporary plot had Fred as Tony Flagg, a psychiatrist trying to teach a radio star (Ginger) how to fall in love with his best friend, only, of course, to end up in love with her himself.

This was a theme to be echoed a few years later by Kurt Weill and Ira Gershwin and Moss Hart for *Lady in the Dark* with Gertrude Lawrence on stage and Ginger in the film. Though *Carefree* pioneered a genre of spoof-psychiatric stage and screen

comedies that ran through to *Harvey* a decade later, it did very badly indeed at the box office (perhaps because it feels the least musical of all the Astaire-Rogers films). It was their eighth collaboration, and now the end did seem to be approaching as fast as that of the decade. Fred and Ginger had made a total of eighteen million dollars for RKO, though that still wasn't enough to save the studio's debts or to alter the perception that the pair's greatest dancing days were already over, barely five years after they had first met on screen.

There was, however, one prewar musical still for them to make, this one totally unlike any of the others. It was *The Story of Vernon and Irene Castle*, a real-life dancing partnership of World War One to whom Fred and his sister Adele had often been

"More screwball comedy than musical" – Fred and Ginger in *Carefree* (1938).

compared. By now, in early 1939, Fred and Ginger had expressed their eagerness to get away from each other. There had been a distinct falling-off at the box office, and above all else there was a limit to the number of times the old formula could be recycled. The Castle story, therefore, came as something of a relief to all concerned. Though it was no more historically accurate than any other Hollywood musical biopic of the period, it did at least have roots in reality. Vernon and Irene had a lot in common with Fred and Ginger. Asked to explain their phenomenal success after coming to sudden fame at a Paris nightclub exhibition dance, Mrs Castle merely noted, "We were young, clean, married and well-mannered." Fred and Ginger scored three out of four on that scale.

The Castles' story was, however, an ultimately tragic one. After their Paris triumph they launched a craze for ballroom dancing, worked on Broadway and in nightclubs, wrote books and even made films about their nimble footwork. In 1916 Vernon, who was English by birth, joined the Royal Flying Corps and fought a brave war. But after surviving considerable hazards in France, he was transferred to a pilot-training programme in Texas and killed there at the age of thirty in a freak accident in 1918.

So Fred and Ginger were not to go out in a blaze of glory, but in a blazing air crash. Moreover, the score for the film contained only one new song; the rest were trawled from such hits of the period as "By the Light of the Silvery Moon", "Darktown Strutters Ball" and "Waiting For the Robert E. Lee".

Nevertheless, as the critic Cecilia Ager noted at the time, this was still vintage Fred and Ginger:

"In *The Castles,* everyone knows who everyone else is. Everybody's identity is clearly

Ginger as "The Yama Yama Man"
(*The Story of Vernon and Irene Castle*, 1939).

defined and completely understood from beginning to end and nobody is mistaken for somebody else, not even on the telephone . . . Miss Rogers does not get mad at Mr Astaire: she likes him from the first moment she sees him and never pretends that she doesn't, and the only change in her feeling toward him is the progressive degree of her passion . . . They're married right off, nobody has to wish to God they would . . . the ending is necessarily unhappy, but there are two actual and satisfactory kisses. And it would take Solomon to balance any more justly the footage assigned to Miss Rogers with that which is assigned to Mr Astaire."

True, Mrs Castle (assigned to the picture as "technical adviser") quarrelled bitterly with Ginger as to the styling of her hair and other matters in which Mrs Castle felt she was not being properly represented on screen. And in the end, as *Time* magazine rather waspishly observed, it all came down to numbers - "Mrs Castle has her thousands of admirers, but Miss Rogers has her millions of hers" - so that, as usual, Ginger won most if not all of their costume battles.

There were some great moments here, not the least of them being when Fred and Ginger dance across a huge map of the USA to denote the Castles' touring dates. But a public already tiring of Fred and Ginger did not now especially want to see them in a story ending with his death, even though, ironically, the factual base gave them both a chance to work more effectively as actors than they had in any of their other films.

In the view of Arlene Croce, there was also a generational problem:

"Through the Castles, masses of Americans discovered their dances and their dance music, their democratic right to elegance and the pursuit of fun. Nothing is harder to convey than the impact of a change that has been universally accepted . . . for more than a generation, America had been dancing to the rapidly changing forms of syncopated music, and it was hard to remember that there had ever been any other kind: in the Thirties the norm had been recrystallised in the person of Fred Astaire . . . more than any other entertainer Astaire bears the imprint of those confident, innocent prewar years. He epitomised the classless, "aristocratic" American of the Thirties, and it is with an anguished sense of his increasing isolation that we have clung to him ever since."

For Ginger, less of a national symbol, more of a working actress, there was also a sense of loss as the filming of *The Story of Vernon and Irene Castle* came to an end:

"This truly looked like the last picture Fred and I would ever do together, and it seemed as if that feeling permeated the whole RKO lot and beyond. 'The Missouri Waltz', was the last number we filmed for the movie, and people were coming from far and wide, even from nearby Paramount and Columbia, along with employees from the front office and other stages in production, to see this last dance. It even got to me - I sort of teared up as we were dancing our last waltz together. This was a very dignified way to end our musical marriage at RKO."

Within two weeks of that 'last' dance, she was already shooting opposite David Niven for *Bachelor Mother*.

> *"This truly looked like the last picture Fred and I would do together."*

CHAPTER SIX

"Miss America Ordinary"

Bachelor Mother was a Garson Kanin comedy for which Niven had been loaned to RKO to do his usual jovial-playboy routine in a silly but surprisingly successful little plot about Ginger being left with an unwanted baby in a department store owned by Niven's family. Kanin's brisk, angular direction ("He's too caustic", someone had once told Sam Goldwyn; "Never mind the cost, get him", Sam replied) and the unusual teaming of Niven and Rogers at a moment when both had sharpened their comic timing and were at the height of their careers, turned what might have been just another low-budget romp into a sleeper hit that amazed even its own makers.

Bachelor Mother was essentially Bringing Up Baby without the wit or indeed the leopard, but it served well enough to confirm Ginger's place at the head of the RKO studio roster. Pauline Kael later wrote that "what makes Ginger Rogers so unsettling, so alive on the screen is her element of insensitivity and the happy, wide streak of commonness in a person of so much talent. Maybe her greatest asset is that she always seems to have a wad of gum in her mouth."

And, away from the constraints of Fred's infinite, weary elegance, it was this strain in her character that she now played out in movie after movie. No longer confined to dancing chic to chic, she was able throughout World War Two to build a separate career which made her by 1945 the eighth-highest earner in the whole United States, with an annual salary of over three hundred thousand dollars. And the films didn't even have to be any good, though one or two undoubtedly were. By now she was also regularly performing them in wireless versions for Lux Radio Theatre.

From there she went into *Fifth Avenue Girl*, a simple reversal of Niven's *My Man Godfrey*, with Ginger as the girl from the wrong side of the tracks who gets hired into a

LEFT With Gladys Cooper and Dennis Morgan in *Kitty Foyle* (1940): "a sentimentalist's delight" (*The New York Times*) and at last an Oscar-winner for Ginger.

millionaire's mansion and manages to transform the whole family into something approaching human beings. Ginger was here alone above the title, as she had so often demanded, but a disappointing box office return suggested that the public at large still preferred her as one-half of some kind of a partnership, even if not Astaire's.

Joel McCrea was thus given co-starring status in her next RKO picture, *Primrose Path* (1940), which took her deliberately down-market, as the *New York Times* noted in some amazement:

"Having long since proved that she can act as well as do the Carioca, Miss Rogers now demonstrates that she has no more vanity

ABOVE & BELOW With Charles Coburn, Elbert Coplen Jr. and David Niven in *Bachelor Mother* (1939): "Miss Rogers displays a surprising ability for enjoying the manoeuvres of comedy" (*The Times*).

RIGHT With Joel McCrea in *Primrose Path* (1940): "The girl who was a dancer in *Top Hat*, an ingenue in *Stage Door* and a comedienne in *Having Wonderful Time* now plays an emotional adolescent with such restraint and verity as to qualify for top Hollywood honors in versatility" (*Life*).

BELOW "Colman and Rogers work together well – a smooth blending of talents and romantic warmth" (*Variety*): *Lucky Partners* (1940) from Sacha Guitry's lottery comedy *Bonne Chance*.

than a Carmelite nun, and that so far as she is concerned when realism comes into the plot, pulchritude goes out of the window. Most glamour girls are willing to ruffle their hair and rub off the lipstick for one scene in a picture for what they like to call 'Art'. But the valiant Ginger goes from this film's first reel to its last looking as if she had strayed on her way to the make-up department and instead spent her time in the greasing pit of a garage. With her normally golden hair dyed black, her enviable figure cloaked in baggy dresses, and her face as shiny as a ship's stoker's, she does an excellent job of acting an underprivileged shanty-town ingenue.'

But not of course for too long. *Lucky Partners* had her swiftly back in evening dress partnered by Ronald Colman, like Astaire an icon of Hollywood debonair elegance, for the

tale of an artist and the girl he takes on honeymoon after winning a sweepstake. This was an old Sacha Guitry script from the boulevard theatre of Paris, and it did not easily survive an Atlantic crossing. But now, and largely by luck, she was to land the role that led to her only Oscar. RKO had paid fifty thousand dollars for the screen rights to a sentimental bestseller by Christopher Morley called *Kitty Foyle* that told the story of another girl from the wrong side of the tracks (this time Philadelphia) who falls in love with a conservative aristocrat. They marry against his family's wishes and she has a baby, but he then divorces her, the baby dies and Kitty finds true love with one of her own background. The aristocrat then returns and a difficult choice has to be made.

When first offered the script, one precisely resembling the kind of movie that Joan Crawford was now making on an almost annual basis, Ginger understandably rejected it as "far too sentimental". She was, however, persuaded by her mother and others to

Getting her Oscar: Ginger with
James Stewart (who won for
The Philadelphia Story) in 1941.

reconsider, and *Kitty Foyle* became a runaway
success despite Bosley Crowther remarking,
in the *New York Times*, on how poorly
Hollywood had altered Morley's original
novel: "the sharpness and the contemporary
significance are missing: his *Kitty* was of real
flesh and blood, whereas Miss Rogers is
persuasive but fictitious. His *Kitty* burned
life's candle at both ends: Rogers burns two

candles, and when one goes out she has the
other always handy."

But RKO mounted a huge publicity
campaign designed to attract the all-
American Miss, on whom, rather surprisingly,
they perceived *Kitty Foyle* to be based: "If
there isn't one in your family," announced the
posters, "there's one across the street, or
facing you across an office desk, or in the

subway or streetcar."

To underline this new image of Ginger as
Miss America Ordinary, they even had her
travel to Grand Central Station to receive an
award from two thousand New York
secretaries. Ginger, to whom the concept of
dressing down was somewhat alien, stepped
off the train in a full-length mink and
diamonds, only to have *Time* magazine
solemnly announce that "Miss Rogers, with
her shoulder-length tresses, her trim figure,
her full lips, her prancing feet and honest-to-
goodness manner, is the flesh-and-blood
symbol of the all-American working girl."

Or at any rate those living in California on
three hundred thousand dollars a year plus
clothing allowance.

The conventional wisdom about the 1940
Oscar was that it would go to Joan Fontaine
for *Rebecca*. The others in the best-actress

frame were
Bette Davis,
Katharine
Hepburn and
Susan
Hayward, and
so the one
thing
everyone
thought was that it would not go to
Ginger Rogers. But, of course, it did. "I
always knew you'd make good," said Lynn
Fontanne handing over the award only a little
patronisingly, and it was then left to Ginger
ritually to thank her mother and announce
that it was the happiest night of her life; also,
perhaps, one of the most surprising.

Now divorced from Lew Ayres, Ginger was
still living with her mother but being squired
by just about every eligible actor in town.

"Me and my GI": Ginger with her third husband, Jack Briggs, in 1943.

"We always knew when Ginger was starting a new affair," said a rather tired studio executive, "because she would come onto the set in the morning complaining that the script was terrible, which was just her way of letting us know she hadn't quite got around to learning it the previous night."

It was a gracious Fred Astaire (at the time unOscared himself) who led the cheering for Ginger when she got hers. Nobody seemed to think there was anything deliberately contrary in the decision of the Academy to reward her for what was by any reckoning not the most inspiring dramatic performance of the year, while having for almost a decade deliberately withheld any formal recognition of her work with Fred. The fact that they had only their work in common, Ginger having gone straight from stage to screen while avoiding Fred's high-society world on Broadway and in the West End, meant that theirs was always a distant partnership. "When you work with somebody all day long for ten movies in ten years you may become

good friends," said Ginger once, "but I was as delighted as he was that we didn't also have to meet for dinner."

When she got her Oscar, Fred's telegram read simply, "Ouch". The man who had once dismissed her as "just a Charleston dancer" now had to admit that she was more securely fixed in the Hollywood firmament than he was. The London critic James Agate may have noted that "tap-dancing is the most pointless activity it is possible to imagine," but there were already those nostalgic for the

return of Fred and Ginger, something they were to be denied for another eight years.

In the meantime, Ginger's reward for bringing home the statue for *Kitty Foyle* was *Tom, Dick and Harry*, a comedy in which she played a telephonist fantasising about life with three very different potential husbands - a car salesman (George Murphy), a garage mechanic (Burgess Meredith) and a millionaire (Alan Marshall). Again, Ginger's reviews were glowing. "No other actress," reckoned Bosley Crowther for the *New York*

ABOVE & TOP A *Lolita* ahead of its time: *The Major and the Minor* (1942). "Miss Rogers has the nerve of few movie stars in playing a gangling twelve-year-old nothing short of magnificently" (*New York Herald-Tribune*).

Times, "has that perfect combination of scepticism and daffiness." Garson Kanin, who had done so much to establish the comic potential of her old *Stage Door* rival Kate Hepburn, was in no doubt that here was another real and rare talent:

"Ginger was just extraordinary. She'd do musicals, mysteries, whatever they threw at her; half the time she didn't have the faintest idea herself. They'd say 'Go to Stage Eleven' and she'd just act in whatever was happening there at the time. She was ambitious and courageous. And she had a mother. When Lew Ayres got his divorce, you know, he said it wasn't Ginger he couldn't stand - it was Lela. She was just always there, watching: on *Tom, Dick and Harry* we had an extremely handsome silent extra called Jack Briggs, and I used to watch Ginger watching him; then I'd watch Lela watching Ginger watching him. A few weeks after the shooting, both Briggs and I were called up into the American army; a few months after that, Briggs and Ginger were engaged to be married.'

Before that, however, she went on to play *Roxie Hart,* the gum-chewing, wisecracking

ABOVE Ginger as (yet again) the Brooklyn showgirl, Cary Grant as the journalist in *Once Upon A Honeymoon* (1942).

Chicago nightclub dancer who takes the rap for a murder committed by her husband, only to be defended by the equally wisecracking lawyer Billy Flynn. If the plot sounds familiar, perhaps it's because the story was originally a Broadway drama (with Francine Larrimore), then a Hollywood silent (with Phyllis Haver) and most recently, retitled *Chicago*, a Kander & Ebb musical directed on stage by Bob Fosse for his wife, Gwen Verdon.

But by now even Ginger's public seemed to be tiring of her as the all-knowing, all-surviving chorus girl with the heart of pure steel, and for the next few months she drifted from studio to studio, turning up in one of the currently fashionable all-star anthology pictures. *Tales of Manhattan*, subtitled "the Story of a Suit". She got third billing to Charles Laughton and Rita Hayworth, directly above Charles Boyer, Henry Fonda, Edward G. Robinson, Paul Robeson and Cesar Romero, a position that gives a reasonably precise indication of her star status early in 1942.

From there she went on to *The Major and the Minor*, Billy Wilder's first film as a director. This was a characteristically subversive Wilder farce about a woman who disguises as herself as a schoolgirl in order to travel home half-fare, falls in love en route with Ray Milland and, eventually, has to own

Variety: "Leo McCarey's main problem as director is a film trying to go several places all at once": *Once Upon A Honeymoon* (1942).

up to her real age.

What, of course, Wilder was making, just twenty years ahead of time, was his very own *Lolita*; but so subtly was it disguised, so slavishly did it follow the Hollywood-comedy conventions of the time, that the code was never cracked. There was another memorable wrinkle in that at one point in the plot Ginger is obliged to disguise herself as her own mother, whereupon her real mother (playing her real mother in the movie) has to become her grandmother.

From those confused relative values, Ginger returned speedily to her old RKO home. Refinanced for the Forties, they were able to welcome her back with an early but prestigious wartime satire, *Once Upon A Honeymoon*, in which Ginger played her old Brooklyn showgirl yet again, but one who is married to an evil Nazi (Walter Slezak) until she is shown the error of her ways by Cary Grant, a roving reporter and more suitable escort. There's a wonderfully black scene on a boat, from which Ginger has hurled Slezak, having ascertained that he cannot swim. She and Cary then discuss at some length how long it would take to get a life-raft to rescue him, before simply deciding not to bother and wandering off towards the fade-out. But black comedy and bad taste get easily confused in wartime, and Leo McCarey's stylish comedy, reckoned in retrospect to be as witty as Lubitsch's contemporaneous *To Be or Not To Be*, was in its time dismissed by all but a handful of critics who were prepared to overlook a scene

> *But by now even Ginger's public seemed to be tiring of her as the all-knowing, all-surviving chorus girl with the heart of pure steel, and for the next few months she drifted from studio to studio.*

of breathtaking bad taste in which Cary and Ginger pose as Jews in order to infiltrate a concentration camp: *Schindler's List* it wasn't.

By now Ginger was spending what little spare time she had making such army information shorts as the rivetingly-titled *Safeguarding Military Information* or the more appealing *Ginger Finds a Bargain,* a commercial for war bonds. By now she had also decided to marry Jack Briggs, whom she announced was "all I had ever dreamed of". This third marriage outlived the war by several months and almost achieved a fifth anniversary before he, too, by Miss Rogers's account, succumbed to the demon drink. She did, however, manage to cure several warts on his feet, by the strict application the self-help principles of Christian Science to which she, following Lela, was now converted.

With a third marriage headed as rapidly for the rocks as the earlier two, a situation not helped by long wartime separations and Ginger's feeling that "he couldn't keep a productive thought in his head" (Briggs's feelings about Ginger and Lela, if any, were never made public), it was work as usual. Immediately after *Once Upon A Honeymoon* came *Tender Comrade*, in which Rogers was a young defence-plant worker shacking up with three other war widows while their guys were at the Front. *Time* magazine thought that watching this one was like being "brained by powder puffs" but the reviewer also called it "the *Little Women* of World War Two", which was good enough for the posters.

CHAPTER SEVEN

"Lady in the Dark"

Tender Comrade was to become a camp classic at bad-movie festivals all over the world, not least for the final scene in which Ginger hears of Robert Ryan's death in action and then holds up his photograph to their new-born baby saying,"Little guy, you two aren't never going to meet. He went and died so that you could have a better break when you grow up than he ever had." But it is interesting for a more scary reason: shot early in 1943, it contained several speeches in favour of communism, communal living and even the USSR, while also daring to be critical of some aspects of American democracy. Only five years later, when Ginger's mother had become one of Senator McCarthy's most savage red-baiters during the witch-hunts, and it was remarked that her daughter had starred in this film, Lela went on the record to say that Ginger had been forced to make it and had anyway insisted

Their last meeting: The Barkleys of Broadway (1949).

that her more anti-American speeches be taken over by the other little mothers in the picture. By 1947, the comrades were no longer reckoned to be so tender.

Life was always safer for Ginger in musicals, and now she landed Lady in the Dark, the Kurt Weill-Ira Gershwin-Moss Hart Broadway triumph of 1941 in which Gertrude Lawrence made one her most charismatic appearances and hits. The show had also been the making of a young comedian called Danny Kaye. Its roots were in the decision by Moss Hart, one half of the Kaufman-Hart playwriting team and one of the New York theatre's most distinguished later directors (My Fair Lady, Camelot), to go into psychoanalysis late in the 1930s to work out his own professional insecurities and, many would now believe, his sexual ambivalence.

From his experiences on the couch, from Ira Gershwin's attempts to build a new lyric-

writing career after the tragically premature death of his brother George, and from Kurt Weill starting a new life in America on the run from Hitler's Germany, there had grown what in later Sondheim years would come to be known as the "concept" musical, but this one was the very first of its kind. *Lady in the Dark* concerned a successful editor of glossy magazines whose problem is, in the show's best number, that "she can't make up her mind". By living out her various and varied psychiatric traumas, she is trying to decide between suitors in what Weill called "little one-act operas which continue the story in musical fantasies while the realistic story stops".

Challenged not only by Danny Kaye but also by a young Victor Mature on stage, Gertie Lawrence had set new standards of scenery-chewing by actually eating flowers during their big scenes. By the time the project reached Hollywood, however, all three had disappeared and there was not only a new cast but also a largely new score. Some of the great numbers had sadly disappeared and were replaced by all-purpose Jimmy Van Heusen standbys like "Suddenly It's Spring", and for neither the first nor the last time, Hollywood chose to declare its distance from Broadway by taking a major stage musical and relentlessly turning it into a minor screen one.

Though Paramount spent a record two

"Slopping over with sentimentality and the most banal sermonising" (*New York Sun*): *Tender Comrade* (1943).

million dollars on the project (of which Ginger, for her first appearance in full Technicolor, got a hundred and twenty thousand dollars), the difference between stage and screen was perhaps best summarised by the fact that, when it came to film Gertie's great number "My Ship", Ginger, on screen, merely hums it.

Lady in the Dark took almost a year to make, was then shelved by Paramount for almost another year while they thought about how best to release an avant-garde psychiatric musical fantasy in wartime. It was considerably delayed even during the shooting when Ginger and one of her dancing partners had to go to hospital, poisoned by the fumes from the dry ice that was everywhere on the set. It was finally released to reviews that were mixed at best: the score that had done so much to revitalise Gertrude Lawrence's stage career only three years earlier now had precisely the reverse

ABOVE LEFT Liza on the couch, with Barry Sullivan as her psychiatrist: *Lady in the Dark* (1944).

ABOVE RIGHT Liza's Dream from *Lady in the Dark*: "governed by special effects and dry ice, rather more than what's on her mind" (*New Yorker*).

LEFT The circus sequence of *Lady in the Dark*, one of the few that survived Hollywood's treatment of the original Broadway classic by Ira Gershwin, Kurt Weill and Moss Hart.

With Gary Gray and Joseph Cotten in *I'll Be Seeing You* (1944): "general honesty and a welcome lack of histrionics" (*Variety*).

effect on Ginger's. Though *Lady in the Dark* actually doubled its investment at the box office, the perception was that, compared to the original, it had somehow been a disappointment, and Ginger's career never recovered. Though she had another twenty years on screen and twenty pictures still to make, with only one, her return to Fred Astaire, did she ever achieve again what might be considered a major hit. Though 1944 would prove her highest-earning year, by that time her career was already on the skids.

From *Lady in the Dark* she went to David Selznick for a routine melodrama, *I'll Be Seeing You*, in which she played a woman who is released from being imprisoned for manslaughter and falls in love with Joe Cotten, a mental patient. After that brush with gritty, downmarket realism she went straight into an MGM remake of *Grand Hotel* called *Weekend at the Waldorf*. This, however, was a distinctly cut-rate hotel package, with Lana Turner, Walter Pidgeon and Van Johnson standing in for Joan Crawford and the original Barrymores, while Ginger, playing the world-weary actress, was predictably no match for Garbo, who had been a ballerina in the original.

1945 brought Ginger *Heartbeat*, in which she rather unwisely agreed to be cast as an eighteen-year-old French schoolgirl when she

ABOVE & RIGHT "Behind the frills, Ginger manages to turn in an attractive and spirited performance in a more subtle role than she usually essays": with David Niven as Aaron Burr in *Magnificent Doll* (1946).

was almost twice that age. There was a limit to what even her most diehard fans could be asked to swallow, and Ginger as a destitute French waif who joins a school of pickpockets on the boulevards of Paris was over and above that limit by some way. Next came a lurch into period costume for *Magnificent Doll*, which had her as Dolly Payne, mistress to both Aaron Burr (David Niven) and James Madison (Burgess Meredith) in a bizarre romp through American Presidential history in which it is hard to know who looks most uncomfortable. Even *Kinematograph Weekly*'s normally avuncular critic was forced to report that "popular appeal will here be jeopardised by

holding up, however, and although she was now down to only one or two films a year instead of the four or five to which she had for so long been accustomed, these were still on regular offer. Having rejected the part of *Sister Carrie* (which went to Rosalind Russell) because she thought its realistic script "far too

> *Ginger was summoned from her ranch on the Saturday, and by Monday morning was in her costume and tap shoes. The old team was back in business one more time.*

radical", she chose instead for 1947 a fluffy romantic comedy with Cornel Wilde called *It Had To Be You*.

It was then that she got what most would reckon the last really good break of her career. *The Barkleys of Broadway* had been announced as a song and dance vehicle for Fred Astaire and Judy Garland, to follow up the immense success that they had recently enjoyed with *Easter Parade*. But just as Fred only got that job because Gene Kelly broke an ankle, so now it was Judy's turn to drop out: the first of her recurring psychiatric breakdowns caused her to flee the set after only a few days' shooting, and it didn't take the writers, Betty Comden and Adolph Green, nor their producer at MGM, Arthur Freed, more than about twenty seconds to think of the obvious replacement. Ginger was summoned from her ranch on the Saturday evening, and by Monday morning was in her costume and tap shoes. The old team was back in business one more time.

For what was to be their farewell, Fred and Ginger were solemnly announced by their

ABOVE "A pleasant but silly comedy": *It Had To Be You* (1947), the picture Ginger chose to make instead of *Sister Carrie*.

OPPOSITE "The Swing Trot" From *The Barkleys of Broadway* (1949): "a couple with incorruptible style who have done as much good for movies as anyone we know…all of us should be thrilled to see them back, fresh and slick, after a dreary hiatus of ten years" (Bosley Crowther, *The New York Times*).

long platitudinous speeches on freedom and democracy", and the *Doll* disappeared rapidly enough, leaving Ginger to remark that she might now be starting to think about politics instead of acting, a statement that led her disillusioned press agent to add that Ginger couldn't tell a Republican from a Democrat.

Instead she took to ranching a large estate in Oregon and, for a while at least, encouraging Lela in her increasingly manic and vindictive anti-Communist outbursts. The marriage to Briggs was still just about

With producer Arthur Freed and (back to camera) Louis B. Mayer on the set of *The Barkleys of Broadway* **(1949).**

director Charles Walters to be "the Lunt and Fontanne of musicals", a reference to Broadway's most celebrated and enduring theatrical couple. Another reference could, of course, be made to Noel and Gertie, though in fact *The Barkleys of Broadway* was not faintly as autobiographical as a later Comden-Green vehicle for Fred, *The Bandwagon*,

which had him as a lonely, sad, old-fashioned song-and-dance man appalled by what had happened to his haunts around Times Square.

There were, however, throughout *The Barkleys*, sly references to Ginger's eternal desire to "go straight", culminating in a scene where she impersonates Sarah Bernhardt reading "La Marseillaise"; this, too, is a camp-collector's dream.

The numbers here were a random ragbag which included, at Ginger's request, a revival of George and Ira Gershwin's "They Can't Take That Away From Me" as well as a bizarre Highland Fling for which both donned kilts and sporrans. The film with which they ended their partnership was their tenth, and the only one in colour. Bosley Crowther provided the valedictory:

"Ginger and Fred are a couple with incorruptible style, and they've done as much good for the movies as any couple we know. Their teaming throughout the 1930s in a series of musical films beginning with *Flying Down To Rio* in 1933, was one of the most felicitous combinations that the screen has ever known, offering a brand of entertainment which had brilliance, integrity and class. And even though it was repeated in such memorable song-and-dance films as *Top Hat, SwingTime* and *Carefree,* the combination bloomed, drawing variety and freshness out of its own unique qualities. That is why it is quite natural that all of us should be thrilled to see it back in operation after a dreary hiatus of ten years. And that is why it is not surprising that the couple should be as fresh and slick in *The Barkleys* as in days of yore."

Not everyone agreed, however. *Time* magazine thought neither Ginger nor Fred "up to the soaring, smoothly-paced routines of the Thirties: they have become more sedate than ever before". Arlene Croce adds, "Rogers had now taken on a muscular thickness in her back and arms that robs her gestures of their former beautiful transparency. It's the body of an athlete, not of a dancer. She was thirty-eight, Astaire was fifty and their numbers are old-smoothie turns: I don't think that in 1949 we could have asked for anything more."

But by now it was all over: Ginger, unforgiven by audiences since she had tried to go up-market in *Lady in the Dark,* was the one to give Fred his honorary Oscar in 1949 for "unique artistry and contribution to the technique of musical pictures". But that technique was already being superseded by *On The Town* and the new Gene Kelly world of reality rather than fantasy in dance. As Pauline Kael later understood, *The Barkleys* was an attempt to get back to an era already well and truly lost with World War Two:

"Astaire and Rogers danced the most exquisite courtship rites the world has ever seen: but they were fortunate. They embodied the swing-music, white-telephone streamline era before the war, when frivolousness wasn't decadent, and when the adolescent dream of "going out" meant dressing up to become part of a beautiful world of top hats and silver lamé."

Or, as Cole Porter wrote in *Anything Goes,* back in 1934:

> *You're the nimble tread of the feet*
> *Of Fred Astaire,*
> *You're an O'Neill drama,*
> *You're Whistler's mama,*
> *You're Camembert*

> **"Astaire and Rogers danced the most exquisite courtship rites the world has ever seen... They embodied the swing-music, white-telephone streamline era before the war."**

CHAPTER EIGHT

"*The way you look tonight*"

To the extent that she had been the nimble tread of the feet of Fred Astaire, Ginger Rogers was already, at thirty-eight, a relic. She was to live another forty-five years, make another twenty movies and twice that number of stage and cabaret appearances, and marry two more husbands, but nothing was ever again going to be quite like it was when she was dancing on a staircase with Fred.

She was, however, never one to admit defeat. Home on the ranch in Oregon she set about dismantling her third marriage, keeping track of Lela's increasingly vitriolic red-baiting speeches, and considering a return to live theatre. If movies were no longer on offer, the time had perhaps come to think about a play for Broadway. For a brief, golden moment, it looked as though the increasingly unstable condition of Judy Garland might land her another winner. When Judy dropped out of Annie Get Your Gun in 1950 Ginger hastily put herself forward as a replacement, only to be told that she now lacked sufficiently "hillbilly" qualities. The role went to Betty Hutton.

"A merry satire at the expense of our new-fangled television" (*Los Angeles Times*): Ginger with Clifton Webb in *Dreamboat* (1952).

Instead, she made a couple of B-to-Z melodramas. There was *Perfect Strangers* and then *Storm Warning*, which Lauren Bacall had wisely abandoned, leaving Ginger to play Doris Day's sister opposite Ronald Reagan in an everyday story of Klu Klux Klan folk in the deep South. After that came a lamentable Las Vegas comedy, *The Groom Wore Spurs*, at which point Ginger, at forty, decided it really was time to try her luck with a play.

Unfortunately, the one she chose was a turkey by Louis Verneuil called *Love and Let Love* that survived several rewrites on tour but barely three weeks on Broadway, though as usual Ginger got credit for her costumes. "No one that gorgeous," wrote Brooks Atkinson for the *New York Times,* "can be entirely overwhelmed by a playwright's dullness." Sadly, the one good line Ginger had in the whole affair was her comment several years later: "The only guy who liked that whole mess was the author, Verneuil. He just adored it, but later he went back to France and cut his throat with a razor, even though he had a beard and did not shave. I always thought that was kind of odd."

1952: With her fourth husband, the French actor Jacques Bergerac, Ginger inspects Juliet's tomb in Verona.

Down but not out after a major Broadway flop, Ginger returned to California to see what could be picked up there. Not a lot. Hollywood was now in its new-realism phase of the early 1950s, the world of Marlon Brando and *On The Waterfront*. There was little room for Fred Astaire's old dancing partner. She played a radio star opposite Fred Allen in one of the five sketches that made up *We're Not Dressing*, this one, in fact, a shameless rip-off of Noel Coward's backstage *Red Peppers*, which she had once played for charity in Los Angeles during the war. Then came a Cary Grant comedy called *Monkey Business*, which borrowed heavily from his

Bringing Up Baby, with Ginger now attempting the Hepburn foil-role. Finally she took second billing to Clifton Webb in *Dream Boat*, the apparently already topical tale of a distinguished college professor hugely embarrassed when some of his wife's old movies start turning up on television. That was it for 1952, not exactly a glowing return to the screen, and 1953 brought little better.

True, there was *Forever Female*, the first feature film ever to have a world premiere on the television that Hollywood so feared. This one was intriguing for other reasons, too: in a plot closely resembling the recently

RIGHT With William Holden in *Forever Female* (1953): "this rates among Miss Rogers' worst jobs" (*Hollywood Reporter*).

BELOW With Charles Coburn and Marilyn Monroe in Howard Hawks's *Monkey Business* (1952): "those who recall Miss Rogers as a once-famous dancing star will find she still excels in that department" (*Motion Picture Herald*).

triumphant *All About Eve,* Ginger played, courageously enough, an ageing actress falling in love with a young playwright (William Holden, already preparing for *The Country Girl*). Moreover, for those of us who believe Pirandello was alive and well and living in Los Angeles at the time, during the shooting of the film Ginger announced her own real-life engagement to the actor Jacques Bergerac, who was sixteen years her junior. "Actor" was actually only one of the press descriptions given of Bergerac at the time of their marriage in February 1953. Others included "lawyer", "law student", "hotel clerk" and "photographer", but whatever he had been

With Cary Grant and Peggy the Chimp in *Monkey Business* (1952).

Ginger was now determined he would end up an actor, and she started to pilot his career through the MGM charm school with all the dedication that Lela had once brought to hers.

This fourth marriage was to last just on two years, and during it they came to London where Ginger agreed to make her only-ever British picture on the condition that Bergerac was given a co-starring role. Variously called *Beautiful Stranger* and *Twist of Fate*, the thriller had a hugely distinguished British supporting cast (Herbert Lom, Margaret Rawlings, Stanley Baker, Coral Browne) but almost nothing else going for it, especially not Bergerac's performance. "It is perhaps better we do not make any more films together," said Ginger in the understatement

of the year, and very soon they weren't making much of a marriage either. Ginger put this down to his infidelities. Jacques put it down to being driven out of his mind "by her boundless energy, enthusiasm and best-of-all-possible worlds optimism". Still, at least for once, Lela was not to blame.

Four down, one to go, and meanwhile Ginger returned to Hollywood for *Black Widow*, a Nunnally Johnson murder mystery which John McCarten of the *New Yorker* did not care for:

"Ginger Rogers, Reginald Gardiner and George Raft are all visible here, and all of them seem to be very tired. Miss Rogers is tired as a nasty actress, Mr Gardiner is tired as the gentleman a lady is keeping, and Mr Raft is tired as a detective. It's a close race,

but I'd say the apathy sweepstakes go to Mr Raft."

By now she was down to one movie a year. For 1955 it was another melodrama of no note, *Tight Spot*, but, mercifully, by this time there was also the miracle of television. In the second half of the 1950s she did Coward's *Tonight at 8.30* (directed by Otto Preminger, with Trevor Howard and Gloria Vanderbilt co–starring), several solo musical specials, a BBC tv drama called *Carissima*, several episodes of the *Zane Grey* and *June Allyson* series, the *Lucille Ball Show* and the Rodgers & Hammerstein TV musical of *Cinderella*.

Her movie career was somewhat less active, though she did go home to RKO to do The *First Travelling Saleslady*, albeit in a role already rejected by Mae West. The two biggest current stars of TV westerns, Clint

Eastwood and James Arness, were also along for the comic-cowboy ride, as was Carol Channing, but that one proved unsalvageable. Still, said Ginger, ever one to keep up a happy face, "at least they gave me back my old dressing room on the lot, even if it was a little dusty."

The next year she did *Teenage Rebel*, a Broadway flop that became a Hollywood disaster, and then *Oh Men! Oh Women!*, which brought her back to David Niven. Dan Dailey and Tony Randall were also in this one, about which the funniest thing was the director explaining how he had signed Niven: "The usual way: you ring the house and he answers himself. You ask how he is. Fine. Then you ask how Mrs Niven is. Fine, too. Then you ask if he'd like to read a script. Love to, old boy, nothing nicer. Then you

With Diana Dors at the Cannes
Film Festival, 1956.

send it round, he reads it, and does the film.
Unless of course he's busy."

Sadly, on this occasion he wasn't, and the
result was another disaster for Ginger. By
now she, too, was proving a lot funnier off
the set, even if usually unintentionally. Asked
at this time by the Los Angeles Matrimonial
Court to justify her divorce claims that
Bergerac treated her with "unreasonable
marital cruelty", she specified that he drove
far too fast, and had the habit of reading out
loud in French to their dinner-party guests.

The divorce was granted on the grounds of
"grievous mental suffering".

By now she was also back on the nightclub
circuit where she had started thirty years
earlier, but this time with rather better
billing. She also toured in a disaster called
The Pink Jungle which closed on the road,
and she took to summer-stock in such safe
bus-and-truck tours as *Annie Get Your Gun*,
The Unsinkable Molly Brown and *Bell, Book
and Candle*.

Producers had now realised that, although

With Dan Dailey in *Oh Men! Oh Women!* (1957): "Miss Rogers excellently suggests a middle-aged wife in search of love, not just companionship" (*Newsweek*).

her singing and dancing on stage were never anything like what she achieved on screen, and although her acting was at best adequate, she already carried a kind of nostalgia value that could be cashed in at the box office, just so long as she stayed far away from anywhere that might have critics of note or refined tastes. Not that working with Ginger now was any easier than it had ever been, as her *Pink Jungle* producer Paul Gregory recalled some fifteen years later:

"Ginger Rogers? She's one of the reasons I left show business. The only other people I ever had to deal with who were almost as rotten as she were Claudette Colbert, Charles Laughton and Raymond Massey. Rogers is a

> "We'd give her a new scene and she couldn't remember the lines. She couldn't sing and, more surprisingly, she couldn't handle the dances when they were not all done in separate takes."

totally manufactured commodity: we'd give her a new scene and she couldn't remember the lines. She couldn't sing and, more surprisingly, she couldn't handle the dances when they were not all done in separate takes. And all through the horror of the show she'd be there, smiling and grinning and utterly unreal. There's no denying her nostalgia appeal to the public: that's what makes her so dangerous. She almost smiled me into bankruptcy. God knows, I don't mind her being a Christian Scientist, but I just wish she'd put a little more emphasis on the Christian."

Bloody but unbowed, she now took as her fifth and last husband one William Marshall,

"Ginger and Fred": The film she tried to have banned in America was a 1985 Federico Fellini satire about an ageing pair of Italian dancers brought out of retirement to repeat their Astaire/Rogers act on television: The stars were Marcello Mastroianni and Giuletta Masina.

an actor-producer-writer she had first met on *Kitty Foyle.* This marriage, too, succumbed in Ginger's view to the demon drink ("he had breath that would have set the house on fire if I had lit it with a match"), but not before the two of them had set up home in Jamaica, where, bizarrely, they thought they could also set up a film industry. The one film they produced, *Quick, Let's Get Married*, was held up for four entire years in financial wrangles and then, fortunately, only ever shown to a very few friends.

But now, and for the very last time, Hollywood beckoned Ginger, though, once again, only because of the illness of Judy Garland. This time the picture was *Harlow*, made in eight days in Electronovision to beat a more expensive version of Jean Harlow's tragic life into the cinemas. Ginger played her mother and lost, to Angela Lansbury, who played the role far better in the rival version.

This was her last and seventy-third film in a screen career spanning exactly thirty-five years. It was followed by an immediate return to Broadway.

By the summer of 1965, David Merrick was looking for a replacement for Carol Channing, who had already played two years of *Hello Dolly!* in New York, because he was now keen to take the show elsewhere. Ginger, having proved herself in stage musicals on the road, was an obvious choice. Indeed, she played the part for another two years and then longer on the road. Of all Channing's many starry replacements, Rogers was said to be the most efficient and the least popular. The director Gower Champion fled in rehearsal, only to run into his old friend and Astaire choreographer Hermes Pan in the street. "But Hermes," he is said to have said, "why didn't you tell me?" "About Ginger?" replied Pan, "I just thought everybody always knew."

December 1968: Arriving in London, with her fifth and last husband Bill Russell, to start rehearsing "Mame".

Yet there was better to come. On the strength of her New York and road success with *Dolly,* Ginger was in 1968 offered a starring debut in London at the Theatre Royal, Drury Lane in *Mame* for which she got five thousand pounds a week and some more terrible reviews: "Not so much *Mame* as Tame" wrote the *Daily Mail.* Again Ginger did not exactly endear herself to the cast or backstage crew, nor on this occasion to the orchestra to whom she solemnly presented one rather small packet of jellybabies as a Christmas present.

BERNARD DELFONT
and
HAROLD FIELDING
in association with
FRYER, CARR & HARRIS
present

GINGER ROGERS
in
MAME

Book
JEROME LAWRENCE and ROBERT E. LEE

Music and Lyrics
JERRY HERMAN

Based on the novel "Auntie Mame" by
PATRICK DENNIS
and the play by
LAWRENCE and LEE

with
MARGARET COURTENAY   ANN BEACH
BARRY KENT   GUY SPAULL   BURT KWOUK
Sheila Keith   Tony Adams   Brian Jackson
and GARY WARREN

Settings WILLIAM and JEAN ECKART
Costumes ROBERT MACKINTOSH
Lighting THARON MUSSER
Vocal Arrangements
DONALD PIPPIN   Dance Music Arrangements
ROGER ADAMS
Orchestrations PHILIP J. LANG
Musical Direction RAY COOK
Assistant Choreographer
PATRICK CUMMINGS   Choral Director
JOHN McCARTHY
Associate Producer in New York   JOHN BOWAB
Dances and Musical Numbers Staged by
ONNA WHITE
Original New York production directed by
GENE SAKS
Re-staged by
LAWRENCE KASHA

THEATRE ROYAL
DRURY LANE
CHAIRMAN: PRINCE LITTLER CBE
Manager: GEORGE HOARE Secretary S.L. DREW F.C.I.S

Ginger on television with Doug Fairbanks Jr. in a 1980 episode of *Love Boat*.

By now, just sixty herself, Ginger proudly announced to the press that her mother was making her first ever transatlantic flight to see her little girl perform at the Lane. When that closed after a year, the two of them returned to America to settle Ginger's fifth divorce and pick up some television work. Soon enough Ginger was back on the road, not so much tour de force as forced to tour, and this time, adding insult to injury, playing dud dates in *Coco*, the Chanel musical in which her old RKO rival Katharine Hepburn had achieved a huge personal success on Broadway.

By now the career was running down fast. There was one more musical tour (*No, No, Nanette*), some straight plays in summer theatres (*Our Town, Forty Carats*); but there was something relentless about all of this, as

though she just would not admit to failure or retirement. Well into the 1980s she was on the road, finishing up in Edmonton, Canada, with *Charley's Aunt* at the age of 75.

Along the way there were occasional television specials and a bizarre assignment to retail her own "Ginger Pantyhose" for a major department store. True to her right-wing principles, she campaigned for Nixon as both California Governor and President on a personal platform of "goodness and morality and cleanliness", though without specifying the order. She also crusaded for Christian Science and won a Freedom Foundation Award from the Los Angeles civic community.

Mother finally went her Christian Scientist way in 1977, but a year or two later Ginger

There was one more musical tour, some straight plays in summer theatres; but there was something relentless about all of this, as though she just would not admit to failure.

A last meeting, backstage after *Mame* in 1969.

was at Radio City Music Hall guest-starring with the Rockettes, and by 1980 she was in Paris at the Olympia doing a solo show that she took on to Buenos Aires. After that she did a farewell tour of *Anything Goes* and started on her memoirs, which were published in 1991 to politely stifled critical yawns. She then made several more personal appearances, not the least of which was at the New York *Night of 100 Stars*. Her last public appearance was in London in December 1994, though on that occasion she was able

to do little more than wave from a wheelchair. Still, she was up there in the lights one more time and you had to admire the tenacity, if not always the talent.

The best story about her, and her mother, that I have ever heard is told by the Hollywood biographer George Eells and it goes as follows:

"During her tour of *Forty Carats* in 1975, an especially devoted pair of fans, brother and sister, bought seats and two copies of Arlene Croce's *The Fred Astaire and Ginger*

RIGHT 1984: Ginger at 73 goes into television for *Glitter*: "My first picture was *Kitty Foyle* – it was my mother who always danced with Fred Astaire".

Rogers Book well in advance. They enjoyed the performance enormously, and presented themselves at the stage door, where a doorman took the books to Ginger's dressing room for autographs. He returned to say that he was sorry, but the star would not sign the books, because they were unauthorised biographies. Determined to have a memento, the brother then shoved their programmes into the doorman's hand and demanded to have them signed instead. Shortly thereafter a commotion out front made it clear that Ginger was leaving by another exit. Desperate now, the young man raced to the street and seemed about to fling himself in front of the limousine into which Ginger was scrambling. Suddenly, from the depths of its interior, a voice commanded, "Be polite. Sign. Be thankful they still remember you." The voice belonged to Lela."

Ginger Rogers, born Virginia McMath 1911, died 1995 at her home in California. Five marriages, no children. She was the dance queen of Hollywood, as they said in all the obituaries, and George Balanchine once remarked that he only came to America because it was a land of girls like Ginger Rogers. Some of the others may have been better dancers; Ginger was a better star. Only with her did dance in the movie musical become a medium of serious emotion, only with her did Astaire do his very best work, only with her did sophistication suddenly become accessible to all:

Some day, when I'm awfully low,
And the world is cold,
I will feel a glow just thinking of you,
And the way you look tonight.

Filmography

FEATURE FILMS

Young Man of Manhattan 1930
Paramount
Director: Monta Bell; Producer: Monta Bell; Screenplay: Robert Presnell, based on a story by Katherine Brush; Cinematographer: Larry Williams; Music and lyrics: Irving Kahal, Pierre Norman, and Sammy Fain. Cast: Claudette Colbert, Norman Foster, Charles Ruggles, Ginger Rogers.

Queen High 1930 Paramount
Director: Fred Newmeyer; Producer: Lawrence Schwab and Frank Mandel; Screenplay: Frank Mandel, based on a play by Edward H. Peple; Cinematographer: William Steiner; Music and lyrics: B. G. DeSylva and Lewis Gensler, Dick Howard and Ralph Rainger, Arthur Schwartz and Ralph Rainger, E. Y. Harburg and Henry Souvain. Cast: Charles Ruggles, Frank Morgan, Ginger Rogers, Stanley Smith.

The Sap from Syracuse 1930
Paramount
Director: A. Edward Sutherland;
Screenplay: Gertrude Purcell, based on the play by John Wray, Jack O'Donnell and John Hayden; Cinematographer: Larry Williams; Music and lyrics: E. Y. Harburg and Johnny Green. Cast: Jack Oakie, Ginger Rogers, Granville Bates, George Barbier.

Follow the Leader 1930
Paramount
Director: Norman Taurog; Screenplay: Gertrude Purcell and Sid Silvers, based on the play Manhattan Mary by William K. Wells, George White, B.G DeSylva, Lew Brown and Ray Henderson; Cinematographer: Larry Williams; Music and lyrics: Lew Brown, B. G. DeSylva and Ray Henderson, Irving Kahal and Sammy Fain. Cast: Ed Wynn, Ginger Rogers, Stanley Smith, Lou Holtz, Lida Kane, Ethel Merman.

Honor Among Lovers 1931
Paramount
Director: Dorothy Arzner; Screenplay: Austin Parker; Cinematographer: George Folsey. Cast: Claudette Colbert, Fredric March, Charles Ruggles, Ginger Rogers, Monroe Owsley, Avonne Taylor.

The Tip Off 1931 RKO-Pathe/
Director: Albert Rogell; Producer: Charles R. Rogers; Screenplay: Earl Baldwin; Story: George Kibbe Turner; Cinematographer: Edward Snyder. Cast: Eddie Quillan, Robert Armstrong, Ginger Rogers, Joan Peers, Ralf Harolde.

Suicide Fleet 1931 RKO-Pathe/
Director: Albert Rogell; Producer: Charles R. Rogers; Screenplay: Lew Lipton, based on the story ``Mystery Ship'' by Commander Herbert A. Jones, U.S.N.; Cinematographer: Sol Polito. Cast: Bill Boyd, Robert Armstrong, James Gleason, Ginger Rogers, Harry Bannister.

Carnival Boat 1932 RKO-Pathe/
Director: Albert Rogell; Producer: Charles R. Rogers; Screenplay: James Seymour, based on a story by Marion Jackson and Don Ryan; Cinematographer: Ted McCord. Cast: Bill Boyd, Ginger Rogers, Fred Kohler, Hobart Bosworth, Marie Prevost, Edgar Kennedy.

The Tenderfoot 1932
First National & Vitaphone
Director: Ray Enright;

Screenplay: Earl Baldwin, Monty Banks, and Arthur Caesar, based on the story by Richard Carle and George S. Kaufman; Cinematographer: Gregg Toland. Cast: Joe E. Brown, Ginger Rogers, Lew Cody, Vivien Oakland, Robert Greig, Spencer Charters.

The Thirteenth Guest 1932
Monogram
Director: Albert Ray; Producer: M. H. Hoffman; Screenplay: Frances Hyland, based on the novel by Armitage Trail; Cinematographers: Harry Neumann and Tom Galligan. Cast: Ginger Rogers, Lyle Talbot, J. Farrell MacDonald, James Eagles.

Hat Check Girl 1932 Fox
Director: Sidney Lanfield; Screenplay: Barry Conners, Philip Klein and Arthur Kober, based on the novel by Rian James; Cinematographer: Glen MacWilliams; Music and lyrics: L. Wolfe Gilbert and James Hanley. Cast: Sally Eilers, Ben Lyon, Arthur Pierson, Ginger Rogers, Monroe Owsley.

You Said a Mouthful 1932
First National & Vitaphone
Director: Lloyd Bacon;
Screenplay: Robert Lord and
Bolton Mallory, based on a story
by William B. Dover;
Cinematographer: Richard
Towers. Cast: Joe E. Brown,
Ginger Rogers, Preston Foster,
Sheila Terry, Guinn Williams.

42nd Street 1933 Warner Bros.
& Vitaphone
Director: Lloyd Bacon;
Choreographer: Busby Berkeley;
Screenplay: Rian James and
James Seymour, based on the
novel by Bradford Ropes;
Cinematographer: Sol Polito;
Music and lyrics: Harry Warren
and Al Dubin. Cast: Warner
Baxter, Bebe Daniels, George
Brent, Ruby Keeler, Guy Kibbee,
Una Merkel, Ginger Rogers, Ned
Sparks, Dick Powell, Allen
Jenkins, George E. Stone.

Broadway Bad 1933 Fox
Director: Sidney Lanfield;
Screenplay: Arthur Kober and
Maude Fulton, based on a story
by William R. Lipman and A. W.
Pezet; Cinematographer: George
Barnes. Cast: Joan Blondell,
Ricardo Cortez, Ginger Rogers,
Adrienne Ames.

Gold Diggers of 1933 1933
Warner Bros. & Vitaphone
Director: Mervyn LeRoy;
Producer: Jack L. Warner;
Choreographer: Busby Berkeley;
Screenplay: Erwin Gelsey and
James Seymour, based on a play
by Avery Hopwood;
Cinematographer: Sol Polito;
Music and lyrics: Harry Warren
and Al Dubin. Cast: Warren
William, Joan Blondell, Aline
MacMahon, Ruby Keeler, Dick
Powell, Guy Kibbee, Ned Sparks,
Ginger Rogers.

Professional Sweetheart 1933
RKO-Radio
Director: William A. Seiter;
Executive Producer: Merian C.
Cooper; Screenplay: Maurine
Watkins; Cinematographer:
Edward Cronjager; Music and
lyrics: Edward Eliscu and Harry
Akst. Cast: Ginger Rogers,
Norman Foster, ZaSu Pitts,
Frank McHugh, Allen Jenkins,
Gregory Ratoff, Edgar Kennedy.

A Shriek in the Night 1933 Allied
Director: Albert Ray; Producer:
M. H. Hoffman; Screenplay:
Frances Hyland, based on a story
by Kurt Kempler;
Cinematographers: Harry
Neumann and Tom Galligan.
Cast: Ginger Rogers, Lyle Talbot,
Purnell Pratt, Arthur Hoyt.

Don't Bet on Love 1933 Universal
Director: Murray Roth;
Producer: Carl Laemmle, Jr.;
Screenplay: Murray Roth,
Howard Emmett Rogers, and
Ben Ryan; Cinematographer:
Jackson Rose. Cast: Lew Ayres,
Ginger Rogers, Shirley Grey,
Charles Grapewin, Tom Dugan,
Merna Kennedy.

Sitting Pretty 1933 Paramount
Director: Harry Joe Brown;
Producer: Charles R. Rogers;
Screenplay: Jack McGowan, S. J.
Perelman and Lou Breslow,
suggested by Nina Wilcox
Putnam; Cinematographer:
Milton Krasner; Music and
lyrics: Mack Gordon and Harry
Revel. Cast: Jack Oakie, Jack
Haley, Ginger Rogers, Thelma
Todd, Gregory Ratoff, Lew
Cody.

Flying Down to Rio 1933
RKO-Radio
Director: Thornton Freeland;
Executive producer: Merian C.
Cooper; Associate producer: Lou
Brock; Screenplay: Cyril Hume,

H. W. Hanemann and Erwin
Gelsey, based on a play by Anne
Caldwell and based on an
original story by Lou Brock;
Cinematographer: J. Roy Hunt;
Music and lyrics: Vincent
Youmans, Gus Kahn and Edward
Eliscu. Cast: Dolores Del Rio,
Gene Raymond, Raul Roulien,
Ginger Rogers, Fred Astaire, Eric
Blore, Franklin Pangborn.

Chance at Heaven 1933
RKO-Radio
Director: William A. Seiter;
Executive producer: Merian C.
Cooper; Associate producer: H.
N. Swanson; Screenplay: Julian
Josephson and Sarah Y. Mason,
based on the story by Vina
Delmar; Cinematographer: Nick
Musuraca. Cast: Ginger Rogers,
Joel McCrea, Marian Nixon,
Andy Devine, Lucien Littlefield.

Rafter Romance 1934
RKO-Radio
Director: William A. Seiter;
Executive producer: Merian C.
Cooper; Producer: Alexander
McKaig; Screenplay: H. W.
Hanemann and Sam Mintz,
based on a story by John Wells;
Cinematographer: David Abel.
Cast: Ginger Rogers, Norman
Foster, George Sidney, Robert
Benchley, Laura Hope Crews,
Guinn Williams.

Finishing School 1934
RKO-Radio
Director: Wanda Tuchock and
George Nicholls, Jr.; Executive
producer: Merian C. Cooper;
Screenplay: Wanda Tuchock and
Laird Doyle, based on a story by
David Hempstead;
Cinematographer: J. Roy Hunt.
Cast: Frances Dee, Billie Burke,
Ginger Rogers, Bruce Cabot,
John Halliday, Beulah Bondi.

20 Million Sweethearts 1934 First
National & Vitaphone
Director: Roy Enright;
Screenplay: Warren Duff and

Harry Sauber, based on a story
by Paul Finder Moss and Jerry
Wald; Cinematographer: Sid
Hickox; Music and lyrics: Harry
Warren and Al Dubin. Cast: Pat
O'Brien, Dick Powell, Ginger
Rogers, The Four Mills Brothers,
Allen Jenkins, Grant Mitchell.

Change of Heart 1934 Fox
Director: John G. Blystone;
Producer: Winfield Sheehan;
Screenplay: Sonya Levien and
James Gleason, based on the
novel *Manhattan Love Song* by
Kathleen Norris;
Cinematographer: Hal Mohr;
Music and lyrics: Harry Akst.
Cast: Janet Gaynor, Charles
Farrell, James Dunn, Ginger
Rogers, Shirley Temple.

Upper World 1934 Warner Bros.
& Vitaphone
Director: Roy Del Ruth;
Screenplay: Ben Markson, based
on the story by Ben Hecht;
Cinematographer: Tony Gaudio.
Cast: Warren William, Mary
Astor, Ginger Rogers, Andy
Devine, Dickie Moore, J. Carrol
Naish.

The Gay Divorcée 1934
RKO-Radio
Director: Mark Sandrich;
Producer: Pandro S. Berman;
Screenplay: George Marion, Jr.,
Dorothy Yost and Edward
Kaufman, based on *Gay Divorce*,
a book by Dwight Taylor,
musical adaptation by Kenneth
Webb and Samuel Hoffenstein;
Cinematographer: David Abel;
Music and lyrics: Cole Porter,
Mack Gordon and Harry Revel,
Con Conrad and Herb
Magidson. Cast: Fred Astaire,
Ginger Rogers, Alice Brady,
Edward Everett Horton, Erik
Rhodes, Eric Blore.

Romance in Manhattan 1934
RKO-Radio
Director: Stephen Roberts;

Producer: Pandro S. Berman; Screenplay: Jane Murfin and Edward Kaufman, based on a story by Norman Krasna and Don Hartman; Cinematographer: Nick Musuraca. Cast: Francis Lederer, Ginger Rogers, Arthur Hohl, Jimmy Butler, J. Farrell MacDonald.

Top Hat 1935 RKO-Radio
Director: Mark Sandrich; Producer: Pandro S. Berman; Screenplay: Dwight Taylor and Allan Scott; Cinematographer: David Abel; Music and lyrics: Irving Berlin. Cast: Fred Astaire, Ginger Rogers, Edward Everett Horton, Erik Rhodes, Eric Blore, Helen Broderick, Lucille Ball.

Roberta 1935 RKO-Radio
Director: William A. Seiter; Producer: Pandro S. Berman; Screenplay: Jane Murfin, Sam Mintz and Allan Scott, based on the play *Roberta*, music by Jerome Kern, book and lyrics by Otto Harbach, and from the novel *Gowns by Roberta* by Alice Duer Miller; Cinematographer: Edward Cronjager. Cast: Irene Dunne, Fred Astaire, Ginger Rogers, Randolph Scott, Helen Westley, Claire Dodd, Victor Varconi.

In Person 1935 RKO-Radio
Director: William A. Seiter; Producer: Pandro S. Berman; Screenplay: Allan Scott, based on the novel by Samuel Hopkins Adams; Cinematographer: Edward Cronjager; Music and lyrics: Oscar Levant and Dorothy Fields. Cast: Ginger Rogers, George Brent, Alan Mowbray, Grant Mitchell, Samuel S. Hinds.

Star of Midnight 1935
RKO-Radio
Director: Stephen Roberts; Producer: Pandro S. Berman;

Screenplay: Howard J. Green, Anthony Veiller and Edward Kaufman, based on the novel by Arthur Somers Roche; Cinematographer: J. Roy Hunt. Cast: William Powell, Ginger Rogers, Paul Kelly, Gene Lockhart, Ralph Morgan, Leslie Fenton, J. Farrell MacDonald, Vivien Oakland.

Follow the Fleet 1936
RKO-Radio
Director: Mark Sandrich; Producer: Pandro S. Berman; Screenplay: Dwight Taylor and Allan Scott, based on the play *Shore Leave* by Hubert Osborne; Cinematographer: David Abel; Music and lyrics: Irving Berlin. Cast: Fred Astaire, Ginger Rogers, Randolph Scott, Harriet Hilliard, Astrid Allwyn.

Swing Time 1936 RKO-Radio
Director: George Stevens; Producer: Pandro S. Berman; Screenplay: Howard Lindsay and Allan Scott, based on a story by Erwin Gelsey; Cinematographer: David Abel; Music and lyrics: Jerome Kern and Dorothy Fields. Cast: Fred Astaire, Ginger Rogers, Victor Moore, Helen Broderick, Eric Blore, Betty Furness, Georges Metaxa.

Stage Door 1937 RKO-Radio
Director: Gregory La Cava; Producer: Pandro S. Berman; Screenplay: Morrie Ryskind and Antony Veiller, based on the play by Edna Ferber and George S. Kaufman; Cinematographer: Robert de Grasse; Music and lyrics: Hal Borne and Mort Greene. Cast: Katharine Hepburn, Ginger Rogers, Adolphe Menjou, Gail Patrick, Constance Collier, Andrea Leeds, Samuel S. Hinds, Lucille Ball, Pierre Watkin, Franklin Pangborn, Eve Arden, Ann Miller, Jack Carson.

Shall We Dance 1937
RKO-Radio
Director: Mark Sandrich; Producer: Pandro S. Berman; Screenplay: Allan Scott and Ernest Pagano, based on a story by Lee Loeb and Harold Buckman; Cinematographer: David Abel; Music and lyrics: George Gershwin and Ira Gershwin. Cast: Fred Astaire, Ginger Rogers, Edward Everett Horton, Eric Blore, Jerome Cowan, Ketti Gallian, William Brisbane.

Having Wonderful Time 1938
RKO-Radio
Director: Alfred Santell; Producer: Pandro S. Berman; Screenplay: Arthur Kober, based on the play by Arthur Kober; Cinematographer: Robert de Grasse; Music and lyrics: Sammy Stept and Charles Tobias. Cast: Ginger Rogers, Douglas Fairbanks, Jr., Peggy Conklin, Lucille Ball, Lee Bowman, Eve Arden, Dorothea Kent, Richard ``Red'' Skelton, Donald Meek, Jack Carson.

Vivacious Lady 1938 RKO-Radio
Director: George Stevens; Executive producer: Pandro S. Berman; Producer: George Stevens; Screenplay: P. J. Wolfson and Ernest Pagano, based on a story by I. A. R. Wylie; Cinematographer: Robert de Grasse; Music and lyrics: Jack Meskill and Ted Shapiro. Cast: Ginger Rogers, James Stewart, James Ellison, Beulah Bondi, Charles Coburn, Frances Mercer.

Carefree 1938 RKO-Radio
Director: Mark Sandrich; Producer: Pandro S. Berman; Screenplay: Ernest Pagano and Allan Scott, based on an original idea by Marian Ainslee and Guy Endore; Cinematographer: Robert de Grasse; Music and lyrics: Irving Berlin. Cast: Fred

Astaire, Ginger Rogers; Ralph Bellamy, Luella Gear, Jack Carson, Clarence Kolb, Franklin Pangborn, Hattie McDaniel.

The Story of Vernon and Irene Castle 1939 RKO-Radio
Director: H. C. Potter; Executive producer: Pandro S. Berman; Producer: George Haight; Screenplay: Richard Sherman, based on *My Husband* and *My Memories of Vernon Castle* by Irene Castle; Cinematographer: Robert de Grasse; Original music and lyrics: Con Conrad, Bert Kalmar and Herman Ruby. Cast: Fred Astaire, Ginger Rogers, Edna May Oliver, Walter Brennan, Lew Fields, Etienne Girardot, Janet Beecher.

Bachelor Mother 1939
RKO-Radio
Director: Garson Kanin; Executive producer: Pandro S. Berman; Producer: B. G. DeSylva; Screenplay: Norman Krasna, based on a story by Felix Jackson; Cinematographer: Robert de Grasse. Cast: Ginger Rogers, David Niven, Charles Coburn, Frank Albertson, E. E. Clive, Elbert Coplen, Jr.

Fifth Avenue Girl 1939
RKO-Radio
Director: Gregory La Cava; Executive producer: Pandro S. Berman; Producer: Gregory La Cava; Screenplay: Allan Scott; Cinematographer: Robert de Grasse. Cast: Ginger Rogers, Walter Connolly, Verree Teasdale, James Ellison, Tim Holt, Kathryn Adams, Franklin Pangborn.

Kitty Foyle 1940 RKO-Radio
Director: Sam Wood; Executive producer: Harry E. Edington; Producer: David Hempstead; Screenplay: Dalton Trumbo, based on the novel by Christopher Morley;

Cinematographer: Robert de Grasse. Cast: Ginger Rogers, Dennis Morgan, James Craig, Eduardo Ciannelli, Ernest Cossart, Gladys Cooper, Odette Myrtil, Mary Treen, Katharine Stevens. *Lucky Partners* 1940 RKO-Radio
Director: Lewis Milestone; Executive producer: Harry E. Edington; Producer: George Haight; Screenplay: Allan Scott and John Van Druten, adapted from the story ``Bonne Chance'' by Sacha Guitry; Cinematographer: Robert de Grasse. Cast: Ronald Colman, Ginger Rogers, Jack Carson, Spring Byington, Harry Davenport.

Primrose Path 1940 RKO-Radio
Director: Gregory La Cava; Producer: Gregory La Cava; Screenplay: Allan Scott and Gregory La Cava, based on the play by Robert L. Buckner and Walter Hart; Cinematographer: Joseph August. Cast: Ginger Rogers, Joel McCrea, Marjorie Rambeau, Henry Travers, Miles Mander, Queenie Vassar, Joan Carroll.

Tom, Dick and Harry 1941 RKO-Radio
Director: Garson Kanin; Producer: Robert Sisk; Screenplay: Paul Jarrico; Cinematographer: Merritt Gerstad. Cast: Ginger Rogers, George Murphy, Alan Marshal, Burgess Meredith, Joe Cunningham, Jane Seymour, Lenore Lonergan, Phil Silvers.

Roxie Hart 1942
20th Century-Fox
Director: William A. Wellman; Producer: Nunnally Johnson; Screenplay: Nunnally Johnson, based on the play *Chicago* by Maurine Watkins; Cinematographer: Leon

Shamroy. Cast: Ginger Rogers, Adolphe Menjou, George Montgomery, Lynne Overman, Nigel Bruce, Phil Silvers, Sara Allgood, William Frawley, Spring Byington, George Chandler.

The Major and the Minor 1942 Paramount
Director: Billy Wilder; Producer: Arthur Hornblow, Jr.; Screenplay: Charles Brackett and Billy Wilder, suggested by a play by Edward Childs Carpenter from a story by Frannie Kilbourne; Cinematographer: Leo Tover. Cast: Ginger Rogers, Ray Milland, Rita Johnson, Robert Benchley, Diana Lynn, Lela Rogers, Raymond Roe, Frankie Thomas, Jr., Edward Fielding.

Tales of Manhattan 1942
20th Century-Fox
Director: Julien Duvivier; Producer: Boris Morros and S. P. Eagle; Screenplay and original stories: Ben Hecht, Ferenc Molnar, Donald Ogden Stewart, Samuel Hoffenstein, Alan Campbell, Ladislas Fodor, Laslo Vadnaiy, Laszlo Gorog, Lamar Trotti, Henry Blankfort; Cinematographer: Joseph Walker. Cast: Charles Boyer, Rita Hayworth, Ginger Rogers, Henry Fonda, Cesar Romero, Roland Young, Gail Patrick.

Once Upon a Honeymoon 1942 RKO-Radio
Director: Leo McCarey; Producer: Leo McCarey; Screenplay: Sheridan Gibney, story by Sheridan Gibney and Leo McCarey; Cinematographer: George Barnes. Cast: Ginger Rogers, Cary Grant, Walter Slezak, Albert Dekker, Albert Basserman.

Tender Comrade 1943
RKO-Radio
Director: Edward Dmytryk; Producer: David Hempstead; Screenplay: Dalton Trumbo; Cinematographer: Russell Metty. Cast: Ginger Rogers, Robert Ryan, Ruth Hussey, Patricia Collinge, Mady Christians, Kim Hunter, Jane Darwell.

Lady in the Dark 1944 Paramount
Director: Mitchell Leisen; Producer: Mitchell Leisen; Screenplay: Frances Goodrich and Albert Hackett, based on the play by Moss Hart; Cinematographer: Ray Rennahan; Music and lyrics: Kurt Weill and Ira Gershwin, Johnny Burke and Jimmy Van Heusen, Robert Emmett Dolan, Clifford Grey and Victor Schertzinger. Cast: Ginger Rogers, Ray Milland, Warner Baxter, Jon Hall, Barry Sullivan, Mischa Auer, Phyllis Brooks.

I'll Be Seeing You 1944 Selznick International
Director: William Dieterle; Producer: Dore Schary; Screenplay: Marion Parsonnet, based on the radio play by Charles Martin; Cinematographer: Tony Gaudio; Music and lyrics: Sammy Fain and Irving Kahal. Cast: Ginger Rogers, Joseph Cotten, Shirley Temple, Spring Byington, Tom Tully.

Weekend at the Waldorf 1945 Metro-Goldwyn-Mayer
Director: Robert Z. Leonard; Producer: Arthur Hornblow, Jr.; Screenplay: Sam and Bella Spewack, suggested by a play by Vickie Baum; Cinematographer: Robert Planck; Music and lyrics: Sammy Fain and Ted Koehler. Cast: Ginger Rogers, Lana Turner, Walter Pidgeon, Van Johnson, Edward Arnold,

Keenan Wynn, Robert Benchley, Xavier Cugat.

Heartbeat 1946 RKO-Radio
Director: Sam Wood; Producers: Robert and Raymond Hakim; Screenplay: Hans Wilhelm, Max Kolpe, and Michel Duran; Cinematographer: Joseph Valentine; Music and lyrics: Paul Misraki and Ervin Drake. Cast: Ginger Rogers, Jean Pierre Aumont, Adolphe Menjou, Basil Rathbone, Eduardo Ciannelli.

Magnificent Doll 1946 Universal
Director: Frank Borzage; Producers: Jack H. Skirball and Bruce Manning; Screenplay: Irving Stone; Cinematographer: Joseph Valentine. Cast: Ginger Rogers, David Niven, Burgess Meredith, Peggy Wood, Horace (Stephen) McNally.

It Had to Be You 1947 Columbia
Directors: Don Hartman and Rudolphe Maté; Producer: Don Hartman; Screenplay: Norman Panama and Melvin Frank, based on a story by Don Hartman and Allen Boretz; Cinematographer: Rudolph Maté and Vincent Farrar. Cast: Ginger Rogers, Cornel Wilde, Percy Waram, Spring Byington, Ren Randell, Thurston Hall.

The Barkleys of Broadway 1949 Metro-Goldwyn-Mayer
Director: Charles Walters; Producer: Arthur Freed; Screenplay: Betty Comden and Adolph Green; Cinematographer: Harry Stradling; Music and lyrics: Harry Warren and Ira Gershwin, George Gershwin and Ira Gershwin. Cast: Fred Astaire, Ginger Rogers, Oscar Levant, Billie Burke, Gale Robbins, Jacques Francois.

Perfect Strangers 1950
Warner Bros.
Director: Bretaigne Windust;
Producer: Jerry Wald; Screenplay:
Edith Sommer, adapted by
George Oppenheimer, based on a
stage play by Ben Hecht and
Charles MacArthur, from a
drama by L. Bush-Fekete;
Cinematographer: Peverell
Marley. Cast: Ginger Rogers,
Dennis Morgan, Thelma Ritter,
Paul Ford, George Chandler.

Storm Warning 1950
Warner Bros.
Director: Stuart Heisler;
Producer: Jerry Wald; Screenplay:
Daniel Fuchs and Richard
Brooks; Cinematographer: Carl
Guthrie. Cast: Ginger Rogers,
Ronald Reagan, Doris Day, Steve
Cochran, Hugh Sanders.

The Groom Wore Spurs 1951
Universal
Director: Richard Whorf;
Producer: Howard Welsch;
Screenplay: Robert Carson,
Robert Libbott and Frank Burt,
based on a story by Robert
Carson; Cinematographer:
Peverell Marley. Cast: Ginger
Rogers, Jack Carson, Joan Davis.

We're Not Married 1952
20th Century-Fox
Director: Edmund Goulding;
Producer: Nunnally Johnson;
Screenplay: Nunnally Johnson,
based on a story by Gina Kaus
and Jay Dratler;
Cinematographer: Leo Tover.
Cast: Ginger Rogers, Fred Allen,
Victor Moore, Marilyn Monroe,
David Wayne, Eve Arden, Paul
Douglas, Eddie Bracken, Mitzi
Gaynor, Louis Calhern, Zsa Zsa
Gabor, James Gleason.

Monkey Business 1952
20th Century-Fox
Director: Howard Hawks;
Producer: Sol C. Siegel;
Screenplay: Ben Hecht, Charles

Lederer, and I. A. L. Diamond,
based on a story by Harry Segall;
Cinematographer: Milton
Krasner. Cast: Cary Grant,
Ginger Rogers, Charles Coburn,
Marilyn Monroe, Hugh
Marlowe.

Dreamboat 1952
20th Century-Fox
Director: Claude Binyon;
Producer: Sol C. Siegel;
Screenplay: Claude Binyon,
based on the story by John D.
Weaver; Cinematographer:
Milton Krasner. Cast: Clifton
Webb, Ginger Rogers, Anne
Francis, Jeffrey Hunter, Elsa
Lanchester, Fred Clark.

Forever Female 1953 Paramount
Director: Irving Rapper;
Producer: Pat Duggan;
Screenplay: Julius J. Epstein and
Philip G. Epstein, suggested by
the play *Rosiland* by James M.
Barrie; Cinematographer: Harry
Stradling. Cast: Ginger Rogers,
William Holden, Paul Douglas,
James Gleason, Pat Crowley.

Black Widow 1954
20th Century-Fox
Director: Nunnally Johnson;
Producer: Nunnally Johnson;
Screenplay: Nunnally Johnson,
based on a story by Patrick
Quentin; Cinematographer:
Charles G. Clarke. Cast: Ginger
Rogers, Van Heflin, Gene
Tierney, George Raft, Peggy Ann
Garner, Reginald Gardiner, Otto
Kruger.

Twist of Fate 1954 British Lion
Corp. (Released in Great Britain
as *Beautiful Stranger*.)
Director: David Miller;
Producers: Maxwell Setton and
John R. Sloan; Screenplay:
Robert Westerby and Carl
Nystron, based on an original
story by Rip Van Ronkel and
David Miller; Cinematographer:
Ted Scaife. Cast: Ginger Rogers,

Herbert Lom, Stanley Baker,
Jacques Bergerac, Coral Browne.

Tight Spot 1955 Columbia
Director: Phil Karlson; Producer:
Lewis J. Rachmil; Screenplay:
William Bowers, based on the
play *Dead Pigeon* by Lenard
Kantor; Cinematographer:
Burnett Guffey. Cast: Ginger
Rogers, Edward G. Robinson,
Brian Keith, Lucy Marlow, Lorne
Greene.

The First Travelling Saleslady
1956 RKO-Radio
Director: Arthur Lubin;
Producer: Arthur Lubin;
Screenplay: Devery Freeman and
Stephen Longstreet;
Cinematographer: William
Snyder. Cast: Ginger Rogers,
Barry Nelson, Carol Channing,
David Brian, James Arness, Clint
Eastwood.

Teenage Rebel 1956
20th Century-Fox
Director: Edmund Goulding;
Producer: Charles Brackett;
Screenplay: Walter Reisch and
Charles Brackett, based on the
play *A Roomful of Roses* by Edith
Sommer; Cinematographer: Joe
MacDonald. Cast: Ginger
Rogers, Michael Rennie, Mildred
Natwick, Rusty Swope, Lili
Gentle, Louise Beavers, Irene
Hervey, John Stephenson, Betty
Lou Keim, Warren Berlinger,
Diane Jergens.

Oh! Men, Oh! Women 1957
20th Century-Fox
Director: Nunnally Johnson;
Producer: Nunnally Johnson;
Screenplay: Nunnally Johnson,
based on the play by Edward
Chodorov; Cinematographer:
Charles G. Clark. Cast: Dan
Dailey, Ginger Rogers, David
Niven, Barbara Rush, Tony
Randall.

Harlow 1965 Magna
Director: Alex Segal; Executive
producer: Brandon Chase;
Producer: Lee Savin; Screenplay:
Karl Tunberg; Cinematographer:
Jim Kilgore. Cast: Ginger
Rogers, Carol Lynley, Efrem
Zimbalist, Jr., Barry Sullivan,
Hurd Hatfield, Lloyd Bochner,
Hermione Baddeley, Audrey
Totter, Ida Williams.

The Confession 1965 Kay Lewis
Enterprises (Also known as
Quick, Let's Get Married 1971)
Director: William Dieterle;
Producer: William Marshall;
Screenplay: Allan Scott;
Cinematographer: Robert
Bronner. Cast: Ginger Rogers,
Ray Milland, Barbara Eden,
Elliott Gould, Walter Abel, Pippa
Scott.

Stage Appearances

1925-28 *Vaudeville Theatres -* Touring the United States
1929 *Top Speed -* New York City
1930 *Girl Crazy -* New York City
1951 *Love and Let Love -* New York City
1959 *The Pink Jungle -* San Francisco to Boston
1960 *Annie Get Your Gun -* New England states

1961 *Bell, Book and Candle -* New England states
1961 *Calamity Jane -* New England states
1962 *Husband and Wife -* Phoenix, Arizona
1963 *The Unsinkable Molly Brown -* Western states
1963 *A More Perfect Union -* La Jolla, California
1964 *Tovarich -* United States tour

1965-1968 *Hello, Dolly! -* New York City and National Touring Company
1969-1970 *Mame -* London
1971 *Coco -* New England states
1974 *No, No, Nanette -* Dallas, Texas
1974-1975 *40 Carats -* Chicago, Illinois
1975-1979 *The Ginger Rogers Show -* United States and world tour

1980 *Anything Goes -* United States tour
1983 *Miss Moffat -* Indianapolis, Indiana
1984 *Charley's Aunt -* Edmonton

Bibliography

ASTAIRE, Fred: *Steps in Time*, Da Capo, New York, 1959
CARRICK, Peter: *Tribute to Fred Astaire*, Hale, London, 1984
CROCE, Arlene: *The Fred Astaire & Ginger Rogers Book*, Whallen, London, 1973
DICKENS, Homer: *The Films of Ginger Rogers*, Citadel, New York, 1980
DOOLEY, Roger: *From Scarface to Scarlett*, Harcourt, Brace, Jovanovich, NY, 1979

EELLS, George: *Ginger, Loretta & Irene WHO??????*, Putnam, New York, 1976
FINCH, Christopher & Linda Rosencrantz: *Gone Hollywood*, Putnam, New York, 1979
FREEDLAND, Michael: *Fred Astaire*, Whallen, London, 1976
GREEN, Benny: *Fred Astaire*, Hamlyn, London, 1979
GREENE, Graham: *Mornings in the Dark*, Carcanet, Manchester, 1993
HIRSCHHORN, Clive: *The Hollywood Musical*, Octopus, London, 1982

JEWELL, Richard & Vernon Harbin: *The RKO Story*. Octopus, London, 1982
KANIN, Garson: *Hollywood*, Viking, New York, 1967
KOBAL, John: *Gotta Sing, Gotta Dance*. Hamlyn, London, 1983
MUELLER, John: *Astaire Dancing*, Hamish Hamilton, London, 1986
PARISH, James Robert: *The RKO Gals*, Ian Allen, London, 1974
ROGERS, Ginger: *Ginger: My Story*, Headline, London, 1991

SATCHELL, Tim: *Astaire the Biography*, Hutchinson, London, 1987
SHIPMAN, David: *The Great Movie Stars*, Warner Books, London, 1970
TAYLOR, John Russell & Arthur Jackson: *Hollywood Musicals*, Secker, London, 1971
THOMAS, Bob: *Astaire the Man, the Dancer*, Weidenfeld, London, 1985

Photography credits

Archive Photos, New York: pp. 10, 11, 13, 14

British Film Institute: p. 84

The Hulton-Deutsch Collection: pp. 12, 78, 85 (top)

The Kobal Collection: Endpaper, half-title, frontispiece, pp. 6, 16, 18, 19, 20, 22, 24, 26 (left), 27, 28, 29, 30, 31, 32, 34, 36, 37, 38, 39, 40, 41, 42, 43, 45, 46, 47, 48, 49, 50, 51, 52, 53, 54, 56, 57, 58, 59, 61, 62, 63, 64, 66, 68, 69, 70, 71, 72, 73, 74, 76, 79, 80, 81, 82, 83, 85 (below), 86, 87, 88

Life magazine: p. 8

Range Pictures: p. 60
Syndication International: pp. 15, 26 (right)